U0803756

21世纪教学活动设计案例精选丛书

小学英语教学活动设计案例精选

丛书主编　禹　明
本册主编　卢福波

北京大学出版社
PEKING UNIVERSITY PRESS

图书在版编目(CIP)数据

小学英语教学活动设计案例精选/禹明丛书主编. —北京：北京大学出版社，2012.3
（21世纪教学活动设计案例精选丛书）
ISBN 978-7-301-20251-7

Ⅰ. ①小… Ⅱ. ①禹… Ⅲ. ①英语课—教学设计—小学 Ⅳ. ①G623.312

中国版本图书馆 CIP 数据核字（2012）第 021980 号

书　　名	小学英语教学活动设计案例精选 XIAOXUE YINGYU JIAOXUE HUODONG SHEJI ANLI JINGXUAN
著作责任者	禹　明　丛书主编　卢福波　本册主编
策　　划	周雁翎
责任编辑	李淑方
标准书号	ISBN 978-7-301-20251-7
出版发行	北京大学出版社
地　　址	北京市海淀区成府路 205 号　100871
网　　址	http://www.pup.cn　　新浪微博：@北京大学出版社
电子信箱	zyl@ pup.pku.edu.cn
电　　话	邮购部 62752015　发行部 62750672　编辑部 62767346
印 刷 者	河北滦县鑫华书刊印刷厂
经 销 者	新华书店
	787 毫米×1092 毫米　16 开本　10.75 印张　210 千字
	2012 年 3 月第 1 版　2022年 12 月第 9 次印刷
定　　价	36.00 元

未经许可，不得以任何方式复制或抄袭本书之部分或全部内容。

版权所有，侵权必究

举报电话：010-62752024　电子信箱：fd@pup.pku.edu.cn

图书如有印装质量问题，请与出版部联系，电话：010-62756370

序

朱慕菊

当今世界正在发生着深刻的变化。社会的发展决定了教育必须跟上时代的步伐，因此，教育必须朝着适应未来的方向进行深刻的变革。自2001年9月启动我国新一轮基础教育课程改革以来，中小学的课堂里正在发生着质的变化，课程改革的理念已在基础教育改革的实践中得到广泛认同。

课堂教学设计是教学中的一个重要环节，是教学的目的性、过程性、科学性与艺术性的统一，不但需要深厚的教育理论作支撑，而且需要适切运用丰富多样的教学方法和教学技术。本丛书编写者长期以来坚持以新课程的理念为指导，对课堂教学进行了深入的探索，获得了有益的经验。

第一，在教育理论与实践的结合上进行了有益的探索。长期以来，教师们普遍认为系统而复杂的教学理论不易被有效地运用于课堂教学中。而在新课程推进过程中，教师们努力学习新课程所倡导的教学理论，并积极探索与实践的结合，特别注重把教学理论和研究成果运用于实际教学，指导教学工作，同时也注重将教师的教学经验总结上升到理论层面。事实证明，理论必须与实践不断结合才能为教师所掌握和运用；同样，也只有经常性地反观课堂教学实践，对其进行深度思考与梳理，才能使教学认识上升到理性的高度。这套《21世纪教学活动设计案例精选丛书》正是积极探索教育理论与实践相结合的产物。

第二，在教师的专业发展上进行了有益的探索。新课程的推进既向教师提出了巨大的挑战，同时也应看到，它更是教师专业发展的极好机遇。教师工作的性质决定了它不是机械的重复。教师既要坚定不移地贯彻落实党的教育方针，同时作为专业人员还必须遵循少年儿童心理发展的规律，谙熟他们的需求，掌握学科教学的内容与方式。在当今社会快速发展的背景下，教师的专业修养也需要与时俱进。因此，新课程所倡导的学生学习方式的变革、教师教学方式的变革，都需要教师在工作岗位上不断思索，不断进步，实现其专业发展。而本丛书编写者正是深刻理解了教师专业发展对于推进新课程的重要性,他们想方设法促使教师对自己的课堂教学进行自觉的反思与总结,引导教师们在理论与实践之间进行反复的“对话”,并将“对话”的结果以课堂教学设计的形式表达出来,帮助教师整理了教学思想,提升了教育理念,促进了教师专业的发展。

第三,在改变课堂教与学的方式上进行了有益的探索。查尔斯·赫梅尔在《今日的教育为了明天的世界》中指出,在百科全书式的知识已经过时、百科全书比老人老得还快的大变革时代里,教师再也不能仅限于传授知识,而需要“唤醒不被知晓或沉睡中的能力,使得每个人都能分享到人们完全能够发挥自己才能的幸福”。因此,改变教与学的方式成为本次课程改革追求的重要目标之一。这套丛书正是以改变教与学的方式为突破口,对课堂教学如何体现学生的主体地位,如何突出知识的建构过程,如何增强学生的情感体验,如何使学生形成正确的价值观等方面的问题作了大量深入的探索。这套丛书中的教学设计虽然侧重活动性,但每一个教学活动的设计都力图向人们反映一种理念:只有将学习任务转化为学生的自我需求,才能真正唤起学生的求知欲望,才能真正激活学生学习的内在动力,才能真正使学生成为学习的主人。

衷心希望这套丛书能够为全国的中小学教育工作者提供借鉴。

2012年2月

(朱慕菊:国家基础教育课程教材专家工作委员会秘书长)

前　　言

禹　明

最近，国家九年义务教育课程标准正式公布了。在总结我国十多年来基础教育课程改革经验的基础上，教育部正式公布的国家九年义务教育课程标准在强调德育领先、坚持渗透社会主义核心价值观的同时，特别强调了对学生创新精神和实践能力的培养。而要实现这一点，我们就要继续转变中小学课堂教学方式，在课堂上尊重学生，充分调动学生的积极性和主动精神，培养学生的批判性思维和学生的实践能力。为了学习，落实国家九年义务教育课程标准的精神，帮助中小学教师转变课堂教学方式，北京大学出版社出版了《21世纪教学活动设计案例精选丛书》，以帮助中小学各学科教师更好地在国家九年义务教育课程标准的指导下，研究课堂教学，改进课堂教学，提高基础教育的教育质量。

我们一直强调教学过程的重要性。因为学生知识的获取，能力的提升，情感的变化都是在教学过程中逐步实现的。教学过程要由一个一个教学活动构成。要想实现有效的教学过程，一定要设计好每一个教学活动，使教学活动符合学生的认知发展水平，符合学生的实际生活经历。在设计教学活动时，要考虑在活动中学生学什么？怎样学？学得怎样？要考虑如何让学生主动学习，合作学习，探究学习。一堂课是否有效与课堂教学活动的好坏正相关，学生是否能成为课堂学习的主人也与课堂教学设计的好坏正相关。因此，研究课堂教学活动的设计是课程改革的需要，是落实国家九年义务教育课程标准的需要，也是中小学教师专业发展的需要。

“21世纪教学活动设计案例精选丛书”的编写不以某一版本的教材为依据。它是根据基础教育课程改革的基本理念，依据国家九年义务教育课程标准编写的。这就使本丛书具有普适性，可供使用任何版本教材教学的中小学教师参考使用。本丛书收集的活动设计，有别于教育教学案例，它是课堂教学中的某个教学环节，或是精心设计的导入，或是针对具体学习任务而设计的小游戏。每一个教学活动设计体现了以学生为主体的理念，而且经过了多年教学实践的检验，行之有效。由于丛书提供的活动类型多样，宛如一个课堂教学活动设计的“超市”，各个学科的教师完全可以根据自己教学的实际需要，任意选用或组合，也可以在现有基础上改造与创新。在编写本丛书时，我们并没有强求体例一致，这样，我们可以保存每个教学活动设计的个性与特点，体现教学活动设计的多元化。对于广大的一线中小学教师而言，本丛书是实用的教学参考书，因为本丛书的作者都是来自教学第一线，他们的教学活动设计就是在教学第一线产生的。

“21 世纪教学活动设计案例精选丛书”是一套“草根”作品，散发着浓浓的芳草气息，而课程改革的春天不正是弥漫着这股清香味么？愿同行们喜欢它，也期待着你们的指教。

2012 年 2 月

于深圳市教育科学研究院

（禹明：特级教师，教育部教师教育课程资源专家委员会专家，教育部“国培计划”首批教师培训专家，教育部九年义务教育课程标准综合审议专家，教育部外国人子女学校认证专家组专家，深圳大学师范学院兼职教授，教育硕士导师）

编者说明

师范院校的教师职业技能培养的严重缺失，课程改革培训中重理论轻教法的倾向，教师职业技能方面专业引领的不足，这些是导致课程改革中出现诸多问题的重要原因。改变教师的教育理念非常重要，但新的理念不是自然而然地就能转化为新的教学设计和行为的。在这个过程中需要专业技能的支撑，比如如何上好讨论课，如何通过游戏使学生掌握英语的时态，如何使学生通过有趣的活动认识数学的抽象概念，如何让学生通过讨论春游的安排了解人民代表大会的议事程序，等等。新的课程理念只有在这些细节的落实之处才能真正体现出来——这就是我们编写这套《21 世纪教学活动设计案例精选丛书》的初衷。

谁是教师职业技能培养的引领者？是那些将自己的热情和智慧奉献给课程改革事业的富有创造性的教师们。南山区的教师们在这方面作出了有益的探索。本套丛书所收集的活动，不同于以往的案例，它是课堂上的一个教学环节，或是一种精心设计的导入，或是一个针对具体的学习任务而设计的小游戏……每一个活动设计都体现了以学生为主体的理念，都已经被教学实践证明是行之有效的好方法。

这套丛书没有依据某一个版本的教材，而是按照课程改革的理念，依据课程标准编写的，这就使得这套丛书具有了普适性，使用任何版本教材教学的教师都可以使用。其中所设计的活动的类型多种多样，宛如一个课堂活动的“超市”，教师可以根据自己教学的需要，任意选用和组合。即便是每本书或每个设计，我们也没有强求体例一致，我们想让每个教师鲜明的个性跃然纸上。这套丛书是教师的实用参考书。

当教师们的职业技能逐渐提高的时候，课程改革的事业就会展现出更加绚丽的前景！我们编写本套丛书的目的，是希望为提高教师的职业技能贡献一份力量。我们也期待热心的读者提出宝贵的意见。

目　录

一、听　说　篇

二、读 写 篇

一、听 说 篇

My Robot

【设计理念】

《英语课程标准》要求课堂教学以学生“能做某事”为目标，采用“任务型”的教学途径进行教学。本设计力求通过活用课程资源，设计学生喜闻乐见的听的活动，为学生营造一种轻松、愉快、和谐的“听”的氛围，从而激发学生积极主动参与“听”的教学活动，培养学生灵活运用语言的能力。

【活动目标】

1. 通过形式多样的任务活动，激发学生听英语的兴趣，并培养其良好的学习习惯。

2. 能听懂“It/He/She has…”句型。

【活动准备】

录音机，玩具机器人，多媒体课件。

【活动过程】

1. 听音做动作，热身激趣

在学生学习了身体部位的单词后，为了复习检查他们对这些单词听的能力，激发他们的学习热情，可先做“Simon says…”的游戏。

T：First of all let's play the game Simon Says.

开始时由教师示范说，学生做；接着由淘汰的学生上讲台说，其他学生做。

T：Simon says point to your arms，point to your head…

S1：Simon says point to your shoulders，Simon says point to your…

S2：Point to your hands，Simon says point to your…

2. 视听结合，有声有色

复习了身体部位的单词和相关的形容词后，接下来借助实物导入“It has…”句型，介绍机器人的外部特征。

T：(出示一玩具机器人)This is my robot. Please listen carefully and then repeat what I said.

T：Look at my robot. It has a small head. It has long arms. It has thin legs.

S1：Look at my robot.

S2：It has a small head.

…

操练完重点句“It has…”后，播放生动的多媒体课件让学生视听。

T：Please look at the screen and listen carefully. After listening, we will do some True or False exercises.

（检查听的结果并给予优胜组奖励……）

3. 听音画画，妙趣横生

T：Now take out a piece of paper and pencils. Please listen carefully and draw a robot. The one who draws well will get a prize.

Tapescript：I have a robot. It has a big head. It has big shoulders. It has thin arms. It has small hands. It has long legs and big feet. It has fat knees. My robot is cool.

（学生听录音画画，录音是逐句读的。画完后，学生在小组内欣赏交流所画的作品。）

4. 听音辨人，活用语言

T：Let's play a guessing game. Listen carefully. He is a boy and is in Group 1. He has big eyes and big ears. He has small shoulders. He has thin arms. He has fat legs and big feet. Who is he?

S1：He's Tom.

…

T：Now let's divide our class into four groups. Do as I do, please.

…

【活动评述】

在听的教学活动中，如果只是对教材的内容进行机械的听力训练，必然会使课堂气氛显得沉闷。本设计以教材为本，但又活化了教材，灵活运用了学生喜闻乐见的游戏、比赛等活动进行听的教学，消除了学生因焦虑、沉闷而产生的听的心理障碍，激发了每一个学生主动参与听的活动的积极性和欲望，在轻松愉悦的氛围中培养了学生的听力和灵活运用语言的能力。

【资料链接】

1. 教育部《英语课程标准（实验稿）》，北京师范大学出版社，2001 年

2. 禹明，《小学英语教学理念与教学示例》，华南理工大学出版社，2003 年

3. My robot, Book 4, *Primary English for China*

（深圳市南山区月亮湾小学　刘小惠）

On the Farm (1)

【设计理念】

活动是提高小学生英语运用能力的主要途径，教师应精心设计各种教学活动，让不同程度的学生都能在活动中有所收获。听力是语言学习和交际的基础，小学生通过听可以大量吸收新的语言材料，加深对所学语言的认识，并在此基础上不断促进说、读、写各项技能的发展。因此，多层次、高密度、有趣、有用的听力活动是学生学习、运用语言的前提和基础。

【活动目标】

通过听懂并执行有关指令、边听边演、边听边选择、判断情况真伪、边听边说等几个层次的多种活动，让学生分辨、认读农场动物名称 horse, cow, sheep, chicken, pig, duck 的单复数及其在句型"There's…""There are…"中的运用。同时，通过与人合作、积极参与，体验学习的乐趣和成就感。

【活动准备】

教师准备 PowerPoint 文件和 word -picture cards。

【活动过程】

Step 1：Warming-up

1. Pupils say the names of the animals they know and imitate their sounds or actions.

2. Talk about the classroom objects to express existence, using the sentence patterns "There are…" or "There's…"

3. Listen to a new song *Old McDonald's Farm*.

在 Warming-up 这一环节里，孩子们说到了熟悉的 cat, dog, monkey, mouse, bird 等动物名称，饶有兴趣地模仿了这些动物的叫声和动作；谈到了教室物品的存在，如：There's a computer. There's a TV. There are six fans. There are green curtains. There are thirty five yellow and white chairs. 孩子们通过自己说说、演演，实际运用语言，为新的学习过程做了热身准备。歌曲 Old McDonald's Farm 能让学生一开始就感受到课文话题，并引起注意从而产生兴趣。

Step 2：Presentation Activities

Pupils look at this PowerPoint picture, listen to the record and talk about the subject："On the Farm".

在这一环节中，静听是主要任务。学生可以集中注意力听，形成深刻的印象，这是建立准确发音和良好语感的基础。

1. Listen attentively without looking at the words.

静听发音。用图片逐一介绍这些动物，教师走近学生，清晰地重复发音，在英语薄弱或胆小的孩子面前多停留，多鼓励。学生静听，回忆并模仿老师的发音。

2. Connect the sounds and the words.

音形结合。将词卡贴在黑板上，标上序号，教师每读出一词，学生根据教师的发音及语音规律，找出所听到的词。

3. Listen and compare the sounds of words ending.

听音、猜测，对比复数名词词尾发音。出示图片，逐一介绍单、复数动物名词的读法。如：horse, horses; cow, cows; chicken, chickens; sheep, sheep; duck, ducks; pig, pigs 等。拿去单数动物图片，让学生猜测老师即将出示的图片内容。

4. (Books closed) Listen to the tape of the text twice. Pupils recall what they've heard and answer the questrons："How many ducks are there? How many sheep are there?" Then repeat after the tape.

听课文材料做回答。

Step 3：Practice Activities

Level 1. Controlled practice

1. What can you hear?

播放 Powerpoint 上单个动物的声音，快节奏地让所有学生说出自己能听到的声音后，再显示文字、图片，进行对照和检查。最后逐一增加动物声音，学生说出句子：I can hear a horse. I can hear a horse and a duck. I can hear a horse, a duck and a sheep 等。这一活动能充分调动学生的积极性，以听促进说。

2. Play the game of Simon says.

听指令做出恰当的反应，规则是只能听从于 Simon。当听到 Simon says repeat "There are 5 sheep"时，学生就 repeat；当听到 Clap your hands 时，学生就拍手；当听到 Simon says "act a duck" 时，学生应做鸭子表演。

3. What's on the farm?

看图片、听描述、做判断，用句型“There are…”和“There is…”描述农场动物。点击 PowerPoint，快速闪过一定数量的动物画面，学生听有关这一图片的描述，做出判断和猜测。如闪过一匹马的图片，学生听到 There's a cow 的描述，这时学生可能肯定这一描述，也可能否定这一描述。这是视、听、说结合的活动。

Level 2. Free practice

【活动评述】

本设计以“听”的活动为主。学生在轻松和谐的气氛里、活泼多样的活动中积极地参与，在各种“听”的活动中高密度地接触新内容，再在高质量的“听”的前提下进行“说”的实际运用，较好地达到了教学的目的。

【资料链接】

1. www.kiddyhouse.com/farm

2. 鹏博士资源素材库

3. 章兼中，《小学英语教育学》，山西高校联合出版社，1996

4.《英语课程标准(实验稿)》，北京师范大学出版社，2001

(深圳市南山区阳光小学　王小珍)

字母组合 ee

【设计理念】

《英语课程标准》指出，语音教学是语言教学的重要内容之一。而在英语教学起始阶段，语音教学主要应通过模仿来进行。因此，在本节课中，教师通过让学生模仿动物的声音来引起学生的兴趣，从而让学生学会一个常见的长音的发音。

【活动目标】

1. 认知目标：让学生掌握字母 ee 的发音及其规律。

2. 能力目标：通过模仿、操练、表演等活动，培养学生的语言表达能力和观察能力。

【活动准备】

录音机，课件，课堂评价卡——“笑脸”，练习纸，贴纸。

【活动过程】

Step 1：Warm-up

Sing a song *Old Macdonald has a Farm*

T：Children，would you like to sing a song with me?

Ss：Yes!

T：OK. *Old Macdonald has a farm*…

全班一起边唱边做动作。

Step 2：Lead In

1. 课件展示动物的图片，让学生用英语说出该动物的名称（驴－donkey），然后叫个别学生模仿驴的声音。

T：Children，now we are on the farm. Look! I have a good friend. Do you want to know him? (Showing PowerPoint“The Donkey's Picture”) It's a donkey! Say hello to Mr. Donkey. Hello，Mr. Donkey! (Hello，children!) And do you know how does the donkey bray? Who can tell me? (Ask some pupils to tell me their own opinion) XX，can you have a try? (Ask him to imitate)

2. 用课件播放出驴叫声，让学生听并且带着动作来模仿其声音（eeyore）。然后，学生以小组的形式评价自己的表现：“黄笑脸”——较好；“红笑脸”——最好。

T：OK，now let's listen how the donkey bray. Everybody，let's act as a donkey. First，put your two hands on your head. Second，shake your hands up and down，and saying eeyore，eeyore. Let me see which group does the best. 学生以小组的形式评价别的组

的同学的表现："黄笑脸"——较好；"红笑脸"——最好。

Step 3：Presentation

1. 播放录音带给学生听，并让学生说出所听到的内容，接着就让学生说出这与驴叫声有何关系(ee 是驴叫声 eeyore 的第一个音)，最后引出该字母组合 ee 以及发此音的一些单词，并让学生跟着录音朗读。

T：Now, children, let's listen to the tape. Then you should tell me what you have heard. XX, can you have a try? (XX：ee) OK, good. The group leader please give him a sticker. 我们现在所听到的这个音与刚才的驴叫声有何关系？

Ss：ee 是驴叫声 eeyore 的第一个音。

(此处重点在于培养学生的观察能力)

2. 让学生举例说出更多发此长音的单词。

T：Can you tell me more other words which pronounce this sound?

Ss：sheep, feet, thirteen, etc.

(此处是让学生举一反三)

3. 将两张准备好的单词卡贴在黑板上，并示范出单词中含 ee 的部分。然后发给每小组一份练习纸，让学生找出发此长音的单词。

(小组比赛)

T：OK, children, let's have a matching game. Look, I have so many word cards. Can you find out the words which pronounce [iː]? For example, I think *ee* in *seventeen* pronounce this sound, so I make a line between *seventeen* and *ee*. Understand? Now, I give each group a piece of paper. Make lines as I do on this paper, and then stick your paper on the board. OK?

(此处的练习对加强和巩固此长音的发音有很大的帮助)

4. 展示课件，播放一首小诗，然后让学生跟着读，接着全班一起带着动作来朗诵，最后分组表演。(小诗内容：I can see a green lychee, above me in the tree)

T：Now, children, would you like to learn a rhyme with me? First, just listen. Then please follow the tape. OK, can you say the rhyme by yourselves? (The pupils practice by themselves)

Step 4：Homework

在家练习此长音的发音。

【活动评述】

新课程标准强调教学过程是师生交往、共同发展的互动过程。在教学过程中要处理好传授知识与培养能力的关系，注重培养学生的独立性和自主性，引导学生在实践中学习，使学生的学习在教师的指导下变得主动而富有个性。此活动设计注意了语音教学的规律性，以学生为主体，采用即时评价的方式，使课堂呈现出师生互动、平等参与的生动局面。

【资料链接】

1.《英语课程标准(实验稿)》，北京师范大学出版社，2001

2. My age, Book 3, *Primary English for China*

(深圳市南山区海湾小学　李　琦)

字母组合 ow

【设计理念】

我们根据小学生生理、心理和认知水平的发展规律，将语言学习与活动结合起来，让小学生在说说、唱唱、做做的过程中，去感受语言、学习语言、运用语言。此次语音教学课是学习字母组合 ow 的发音。如果直接呈现、板书、带读，使学生熟读后强记其发音，学生势必感到枯燥，记忆效果也不好，更别说能学以致用了。因此，我们设计了这样一节融合了音乐与美术的做中学式的语音课。

【活动目标】

1. 知道字母组合 ow 的一种读音[au]，并正确发音。

2. 读单词时能正确发音，语音标准。

3. 培养学生大声、流利、准确的朗读技能，帮助学生建立分析新词读音的信心，从而实现独立朗读。

4. 流畅朗读韵文，有能力的学生自己创作韵文小诗。

【活动准备】

1. 教师准备一幅大挂图，上画雪景：雪人，覆着皑皑白雪的房子，披着厚雪的松树。（也可用课件呈示）

2. 学生自己准备彩笔。

【活动过程】

在小学生开始学习英语时，将英语学科与其他学科，特别是与艺术和体育学科融合在一起是十分必要的。在小学英语教学中，运用学科融合的思想组织教学是十分有效的。

1. 展示图片的美，引出发音。

T：What's the weather like today?

Ss：It's hot.

T：Do you like hot days?

Ss：No，I don't.（Some may say：Yes，I do）

T：I don't like hot days. But I like cold days. Now look at the screen. What's the weather like?

屏幕上呈现出一幅雪花飘飘的图片，上有一雪人，有覆着皑皑白雪的房子，还有披着厚雪的松树。

Ss：It's cold.

T：Yes, it's cold. Look, it's snowing. Can you see the snow?

Ss：Yes.（教师板书：ow— snow，并带读）
[au]

T：I can see a snowman. It's white. What else can you see?

Ss：I can see a house. There's a window.

T：Great! There's a window.（在 snow 的下面板书 window，并带读）What colour is the snow, boys and girls?

Ss：It's white.

T：What colour is the window, can you guess?

Ss：It's…

直到学生猜出黄色为止。教师用课件着色，使窗户变成黄色，板书 yellow，并带读。

2. 读一读，涂一涂。

听录音，跟读 ow—[au]，snow，yellow，window 及韵文“Look at the snow on the yellow window”。

教师带读一遍。学生以小组的形式齐读，并独立把课文图片中的 window 涂成黄色，然后自己朗读。教师进行巡视，帮助学生检查及更正。

3. 感受音乐的旋律，创造韵文。

学生熟读后，教师进一步引导学生观察图片，并以小组的形式一起创造韵文。如：

Snow, snow
Falls slow
On my window
That is yellow.

【活动评述】

语音教学本是枯燥无味的，但是通过教师的巧妙设计，学生却能从学习的过程中得到美的享受，并发展思维创造能力。

【资料链接】

1. 龚亚夫、罗少茜，《任务型语言教学》，人民教育出版社，2003 年

2. 禹明，《小学英语教学理念与教学示例》，华南理工大学出版社，2003 年

（深圳市南山区珠光小学　余林秀）

Helping Tourists

【设计理念】

我们将复习课的所有学习内容设计成为一个问答比赛的形式(有感于电视节目的问答有奖游戏),并力求体现课改理念:

1. 要面向全体学生,注重素质教育。
2. 以学生为主体,学生互动面要大。
3. 培养学生活学活用,解决实际情况的能力。

【活动目标】

1. 通过问答比赛,让学生互出问题(新旧内容均可),检测近几年来已学内容的掌握情况。
2. 让学生能更准确、更深刻地掌握好本课的学习内容,能区别 left 与 right 的实际方向,能用英语进行问路和指引路向。
3. 培养学生听、说、读、写的能力,特别是“听”的即时理解能力。

【活动准备】

1. 小纸张(卡片状)数十张。
2. 在课前把卡片纸分发给学生,要求学生在自己的卡片上写出一道以上的问题。
3. 老师根据实际情况,针对本课的知识点,也适量地提出一些问题、命令、情景对话等等。
4. 红星帖纸、单词图片和两张小白板。

【活动过程】

先让学生对课文做一个简单、有趣的复习过程,接着才进行紧张刺激的比赛活动,好让他们有一个自然过渡的准备,让他们有胜利的信心和高昂的积极性。

Step 1: words

1. 让数名学生手拿单词图片,邀请一名学生做小老师任意说出其中一个,拿着这张单词图片的那个学生把图片举起来,以此表明他能听懂所读单词。
2. 列举一些拼写形式相象或发音相似的单词(如:station, stadium; airport, apple; street, straight; bus, but),让学生做听音判断的练习。
3. 让学生听音并画出所听到的内容,例如:老师读 Bus No. 106,学生听了以后必须画出一辆标有“106”数字的大巴。

Step 2：Sentences

1. 教师不发出声音地读，让学生观察教师的口形，全神贯注地“听”，“听”出的同学则大声读出来。

2. 将学生分成 A、B 两大组，让他们交替进行读与听的练习。由于学生都有相互比较的心理，这样分组交替进行能得到更好的效果。

Step 3：Competition

1. 把学生分成男、女两大组，称之为 Red Team 和 Blue Team。各小组派出一名队员前来抽出由学生制作的互问卡片各一张，并任意挑选对方的一名同学起来作答，回答正确的组能得到一颗星星贴纸。邀请 10～16 个同学即可，因为这只是比赛的第一回合，精彩的还在后面。

2. 第二回合：回答老师的问题、命令或情景对话。要求被选中的学生通过认真倾听老师说出的各种问题后，立即做出相应的答案。(有的问题是小组合作题，需给予适量的准备时间)例如：

(1) Please stand up and turn left.

(2) Write “Excuse me” on the blackboard.

(3) Can you finish this sentence? Turn left ______ the library.

(4) You want to go to the Train Station. But you do not know the way. What will happen?

(5) Please put your left hand on your right ear, and put the right hand on the left ear.

3. 第三个回合则是放松游戏：让两大组进行悄悄话听力比赛，看哪一组能听得最多、最准。游戏方法是这样的：先请各小组派一名队员上前看老师手中的卡片(都是剩余的学生互问卡片)，接着让两位队员回到自己的组里进行传话比赛，而老师则会随时说“stop”，要求最后听到传话内容的那位同学必须以最快的速度写出所听到的内容。

【活动评述】

虽然游戏简单，却能激发起学生的兴趣，也能培养学生的听、说、读、写能力，尤其是听力。学生参与活动的积极性很高，互动面也特别的大，课堂气氛十分活跃，较好地体现了课改的理念和精神。“生活中缺少的不是美，而是发现。”其实在我们平时的教学生活当中，往往就是你的那一点点突发奇想，你的那一刹那心血来潮，你的那一丝丝灵感所动而给你的教学带来一次又一次的意外惊喜。

【资料链接】

1. 《英语课程标准(实验稿)》，北京师范大学出版社，2001

2. Helping tourists, Book 8, *Primary English for China*

(深圳市南山区白芒小学　陈雪梅)

At Home (1)

【设计理念】

家是学生非常熟悉的环境，在教授课程时，我们尽可能多用情景式教学模式和游戏教学法，让学生在特定的“家”的情景和轻松的游戏中脱口而出流利的英语，从而达到教学的目的。

【活动目标】

1. 学生掌握各个房间的正确拼读和拼写。
2. 学生能灵活运用重点句型，并清楚其运用的场合和语气：
   What are you doing? I am cooking.
   Where are you? I am in the bedroom.
3. 学生能模仿文中对话，并在一定的情景中进行交际。
4. 学生能在所学的知识点上发挥想像力和创造力，并使口语表达的能力得到提高。

【活动准备】

1. 教师准备一幅公寓的平面图和配套的单词卡片。
2. 教师在黑板上画三棵苹果树，根据学生实际人数决定小组的个数。
3. 学生准备一幅自画房间图，标志好各个房间的名称。
4. 与课文配套的游戏软件。

【活动过程】

Step 1：Warm-up

1. Song：If you are happy

T：Stand up，boys and girls！Let's sing a song…

2. Do as I do！（教师做动作并表达，引导学生边做边说：“Me，too”）

教师做睡觉状，并用低缓语调说：“I'm tired.”

引导学生说：“Me，too. Let's sleep.”

教师做笑脸状，并用欢快语调说：“I'm happy.”

引导学生说：“Me，too. Let's sing.”

教师做干渴状，并说：“I'm thirsty.”

引导学生说：“Me，too. Let's drink.”

教师手摸肚子，并说：“I'm hungry.”

引导学生说："Me,too. Let's eat."

Step 2: Revision and Presentation

1. Competition in groups

教师指着黑板上的三棵苹果树说："There're three apple trees: red, green and yellow, for Groups 1,2 and 3. Now I want you to say as many words as you can. One word for an apple. See which group is the winner."

让学生以竞赛的形式说出在先前课文中学过的单词，说对一个单词在其组的苹果树上加一颗苹果以示奖励。

2. Presentation

T: You're so good! But I am so tired now. What about you? (引导学生说 Me too) Then let's go to my home!

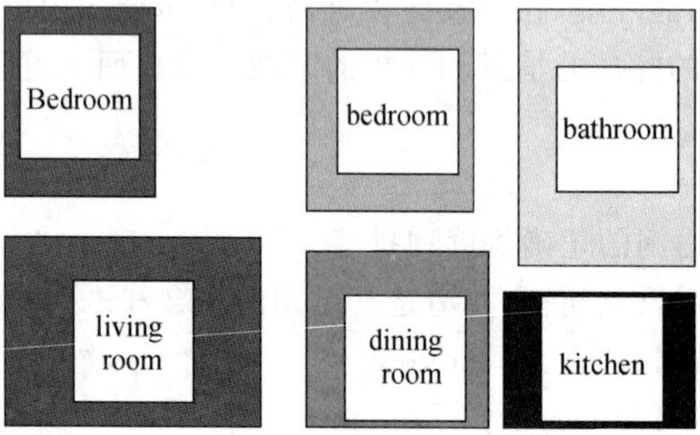

T: This is my home. It's so nice, isn't it?

T: If I am tired, where am I? Ss: Bedroom!

T: If I am hungry, where am I? Ss: Dining room!

T: If I am dirty, where am I? Ss: Bathroom!

T: If I want to watch TV, Where am I? Ss: Living room!

T: If I want to cook, where am I? Ss: Kitchen!

教师边说边做动作，待学生猜出单词后，翻开图上覆盖的单词卡片。

Step 3: Pattern Drills and Dialogue Teaching

1. 教师指着一个学生说："Lily, Where are you? What are you doing?"用肢体语言引导学生说出："I'm in the classroom. I'm having an English class."

2. 让学生以对话接龙的形式操练重点句型：Where are you? What are you doing?

(1) Group work：让学生以两两对话的形式进行组与组之间的竞赛活动。

(2) T: You are so clever. Now, I want to see your home.

(请学生介绍自己所画的图)

学生拿着自己的图到展示台，说："This is my home."

全班齐问："Where are you?"

学生指着图回答："I'm in the bedroom."

全班齐问："What are you doing?"

学生回答："I'm sleeping."

(大概需要五个同学介绍)

Step 4: Reading Practice

教师放录音，让学生先听对话并跟读，然后分角色朗读。

Step 5: Communicative practice

Role play: 英语短剧表演

让学生自由组合分成几组，根据课文的内容，自编短剧。

Peter: Hi, Lily. Welcome to my home!

Lily: Thank you, Peter. Oh, how nice!

Peter: This is my brother, Sam.

Lily: Hello, Sam.

Sam: Hello!

Lily: What are you doing, Sam?

Sam: I'm watching TV.

【活动评述】

运用情景和游戏教学法，使学生在接近现实生活的情景中学习，在学中乐，在乐中学，充分调动了学生的积极性和热情，大大提高了学生的口语表达能力和自我表现的动力。

【资料链接】

《KOKO爱英语》(小学英语朗文版)，世图音像电子出版社。

(北大附中深圳南山分校　廖小芳)

Shapes

【设计理念】

以不同方式的竞赛活动贯穿整个教学过程，从设计单个形状的活动拓展到由多种、多个形状组成的活动，由简单到复杂，层层深入，最后让学生结合实际生活，展开联想，用 triangle，square，circle，star 等形状设计成一件件生活用品，并进行描述。这些活动让学生既动脑动手，还动口，有利于培养学生用英语思维和表达知识的能力，也有利于培养学生之间的合作和竞争意识，更增强了课堂教学的趣味性。

【活动目标】

1. 学生能用学过的句型和单词描述以下图形：triangle，square，star，circle，etc.
2. 学生感受英语和我们生活的密切相关，并学会用英语表达用形状组合的东西。
3. 拓展学生的思维空间，使学生能把学过的知识运用到新知识中去。
4. 激发学生的想像空间，使学生能用形状制作东西点缀自己的生活。

【活动准备】

1. 学生课前剪一些五颜六色的形状图片，带上剪刀和胶水。
2. 教师把全班学生分成四人小组。
3. 教师课前制作一些由多彩的不同形状组成的图片，为每位学生准备一张白纸。
4. 教师制作好的课件。

【活动过程】

1. 剪纸学单词

老师边剪图形边问："What am I cutting?"

学生猜教师剪的东西："Is this a…?"引出单词教学。

2. 比赛描述形状

在屏幕上依次展示图形卡片：star，triangle，square，circle 等。让学生用学过的句型造句，造句最多的那一组获胜。例如：

S1：It's a yellow star.
S2：The star is yellow.
S3：Whose star is it?
S4：I have a star.

3. 考考记忆力

(1) 把每个形状做成幻灯片，每一次在屏幕上快速展示一张。教师先做示范，提问

题，学生做回答。例如：

What colour is this?

How many stars can you see?

What do I have?

Where is the star?

Is the star big?

Whose star is this?

(2) 学生以小组的形式进行问答练习。

4. 看谁最棒

(根据录音的描述，判断这是谁的图画)

T：The children on the screen can't find their pictures. Listen carefully and help the children choose the correct picture.

Listening materials：

My picture has two triangles, one circle and three stars.

In my picture, you can see five squares, one circle and one triangle.

My picture has three squares, seven triangles and four circles.

In my picture, there are three stars, two circles and six triangles.

Four pictures on the screen：

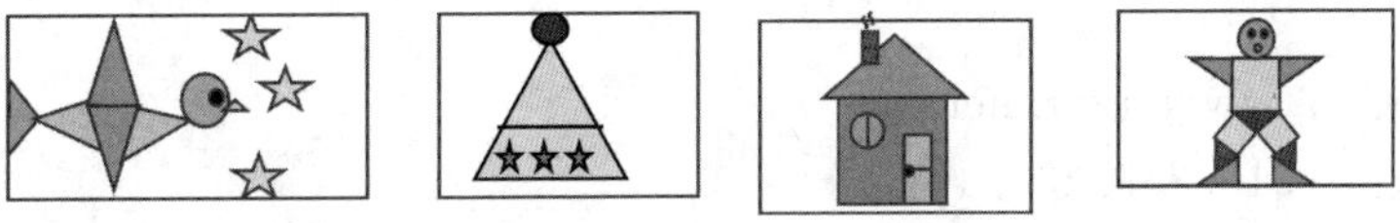

(1) Discuss the answers in a group of four.

(2) Dialogue.

S1：Whose picture is this?

S2：It's Sue's picture.

S3：Yes. Sue's picture has two triangles, three stars and a circle.

The triangles are yellow. The stars are green. The circle is red.

5. 动手做一做

(1) 全班根据教师的描述画出图形。

I have three pictures.

This is my first picture. There are two circles in it. One is big and it's yellow. It's on the left. The other is small and it's green. It's on the right.

…

（教师可根据学生的实际水平设计材料）

（2）小组活动：看谁做得最好。

6. 联系生活，发挥想像

以小组竞争的方式说出什么东西像三角形，什么东西像正方形……

例如：

The moon is like a circle.

My desk is a rectangle.

The national flag has five stars.

7. 制作与交流

四人小组用带来的形状图片制作东西，并在课堂上进行交流。

（学生的作品展示）

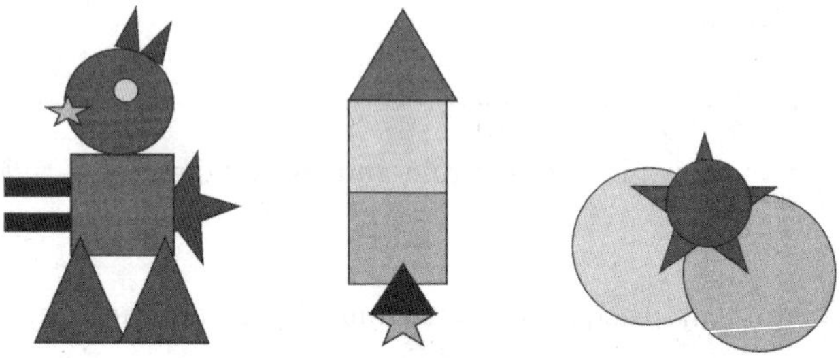

【活动评述】

在课堂上，学生是主动地吸收还是被动地接受知识、学生有没有自我展现的机会，都主要取决于教师对教材的理解、处理程度及备课的充分程度。因此，在设计教学活动时，要以启发、诱导、示范为主，让学生有更多的时间展现自我，并在教好课本内容的基础上旁征博引，开发学生的思维，引导他们多角度、多方面地去学习同一个知识点。利用现学知识，结合已学知识去创造、去探索，培养学生的创新思维，增强学生的创新意识。

【资料链接】

1. http：// www.jggz.net
2. http：//219.239.238.40
3. http：//www.nhsyxxx.com
4. Fun with shapes，Book 5，*Primary English for China*

（深圳市南山区大新小学　蔡若英）

Birthday Party (1)

【设计理念】

美国著名的教育家杜威说：教育即生活，生活即教育。课程标准指出，英语课程要力求合理利用和积极开发课程资源，给学生提供贴近生活、贴近时代的丰富而又健康的学习内容。

“在玩中学。”西方教育尤其注重教育的情景性，强调儿童在学习中的快乐和主动。这也是我去年在加拿大学习、培训的深切感受。鉴于此，回国之后，我致力于课堂教学的开放性和多元化，内容上注重生活化和实用性，学习方式上注重培养学生的自主与合作，并通过对加拿大的生活和文化的介绍，激发学生对中西文化的探究兴趣。

【活动目标】

通过创设生日 Party 这个生活情境，期望达到以下目标：

1. 激发学习兴趣，提高学生的口语表达能力。

2. 了解、比较中西方文化，激发探究西方文化的兴趣。

3. 在活动中渗透人文教育，培养学生的合作意识，激发学生对生活的无比热爱。

【 活动准备】

每个学生带上自己喜欢吃的水果、糖果、蛋糕、饼干等以及往年的生日照片；老师准备六个小生日蛋糕、一个大生日蛋糕、动物头饰和自己的生日照片及多种多媒体设备等。

【活动过程】

Step 1：Warm-up

Sing an English song：Happy Birthday!

Step 2：Lead In

T：Do you know whose birthday it is today?

Ss：My birthday is on… My birthday is…

Peter：It's my birthday today，Miss Chen!

T：Today is Peter's Birthday. Let's have a Birthday Party for Peter，Ok?

Ss：That 's a good idea!

Step 3：Presentation

T：Do you know how to say“生日快乐” in English?

Ss：Happy Birthday!（ 老师板书在黑板上）

T：What's the English for “祝你生日快乐”?

Ss: Happy Birthday to you!（老师板书在黑板上）

The same as this, the teacher presents other key words and key patterns on the blackboard, such as birthday cakes, cookies, I like…, I don't like…, I have a good wish for… I wish… I can get some gifts. I can give the presents to others…

Step 4: Practice

1. Demonstration

T: Peter, please say something about your birthday.

Peter: Today is my birthday. My birthday is on 12th March. Now I am ten years old. I like my birthday party. I like the birthday cake. I also like fruits, sweats and icecream. I am glad to have a birthday party with the teacher and my classmates. Thank you all very much.

T: Perfect!

2. Pair work

T: Now let's do pair work. Please say something about your birthday in English, such as When is your birthday? Where are you going to have your birthday party? What are you going to do?

3. Dialogue

Teacher may ask one or two pairs to show their dialogue.

Step 5: Birthday Introduction

T: Boys and girls, would you like to listen to me about my birthday in Canada? (Then the teacher told the story and showed the photos taken in Canada)

老师先是用英语介绍，然后用中文翻译，大约是这样的：老师的生日是 11 月 18 日，当时在国外学习，生活节奏快，老师几乎忘了自己的生日，是国外寄宿家庭提醒了老师，并为老师举办了一次难忘的生日 Party。Party 上有丰盛的 Dinner：turkey, beef, rice, potato，可口的、大大的 birthday cake；漂亮的 gifts 和 cards；还有 sweet kisses 等。寄宿家庭很友好。

T: Would you like to watch the teacher's birthday photos?

The pupils watched and enjoyed themselves. The teacher enjoyed herself, too. 然后，老师又将孩子们往年的生日照片进行展示，让学生们比较中西方的文化和习俗。老师引导，学生分辨其异同。

Step 6: Discussion

T: Now let's divide our class into six groups. Let's think: how to have a birthday party?

老师将全班分成六小组，每组自选一个同学过生日，看哪组的庆贺方式与众不同，意在让学生融合中西方生日习俗。每小组为一个家庭，老师给每小组一个小生日蛋糕和几个动物头饰，小朋友们戴上动物头饰组成一个个动物家庭，并邀请好朋友们一起参加，即兴表演生日 Party。

Step 7: Birthday Party

T: Boys and girls, whose birthday is it today? It's Peter's. Let's sing Happy

Birthday's song for Peter and have a birthday Party for him.

Ss：OK!

The Pupils and the teacher hold a big party for Peter. They have good wishes for Peter. They eat cakes, sing songs and dance happily. The whole classroom is filled with the song.

【活动评述】

本活动将生活情景再现课堂，有效地进行英语口语的训练。设计之精，教学之妙在于以下三点：

1. 合理有效地开发了生活中的教学资源，教学内容贴近生活。

2. 融学习于活动中，让学生在活动中感悟、训练、运用语言。

3. 课堂自始至终洋溢着浓郁的人文关怀，既关注学习方式的自主合作与探究，又关注学习内容的积极健康。使学生在自主、合作、探究中感受生活的美好和学习的快乐。

【资料链接】

1.《英语课程标准(实验稿)》，北京师范大学出版社，2001

2. 梁祝、卢福波，《小学英语新课程教学案例》，广东高等教育出版社，2003

3. 禹明，《小学英语教学理念与教学示例》，华南理工大学出版社，2003

4. 禹明，《探索新型的英语教学》，四川文艺出版社，2001

(深圳市南山区月亮湾小学　陈飞跃)

Our Fashion Show (1)

【设计理念】

通过活动教会学生获取、处理和使用信息，并用英语与他人交流，发展他们用英语解决实际问题的能力。所设计的教学活动不仅用于课堂教学，还能延伸到课堂之外的学生学习和生活之中。

【活动目标】

学生能自如地用英语描述人们的穿着，并表达自己的喜好。

【活动准备】

1. 教师准备一张图片(图片中有着不同颜色、不同款式服装的人物)。

2. 教师和学生分别准备各自的照片。

3. 在开展下述教学活动前，学生已能认并用英语说出一些服装和颜色的名称，如：cap，hat，scarf，blouse，T-shirt，sweater，coat，jacket，trousers，jeans，shorts，socks，shoes，red，pink，yellow，orange，blue，green，white，grey，black，brown，purple 等。

【活动过程】

1. 教师可指着一些服饰的图片、教师或学生的服装，让学生用英语说出它们的名称和颜色，既复习了以前所学的知识，也为新课做了铺垫。

2. 出示一张图片，描述图中人物的衣着。教师先示范：Number 60 is wearing a pink dress. Number 60 is wearing purple socks and pink shoes. 教师鼓励同学大胆说出图中其他人物的衣着。

3. 结合图片上的其他信息进行问答句型的教学。教师先示范：Who's wearing the pink dress? That's Pat. I like her pink dress.(此句型涉及到表达个人喜好)鼓励学生与老师就图片信息进行英语口语问答练习。经过几组这样的练习，确定学生都熟悉了句型及操练的方式后，就让他们展开 free talk(一种让学生分组口头操练英语的教学组织形式)。

4. 师生共唱一首有关颜色的歌曲，活跃课堂气氛。

5. 教师示范介绍自己的照片，鼓励学生拿出自带的照片做自我介绍。大家先 free talk，然后再单独走上台来介绍自己的照片。

【活动评述】

活动设计注意遵循语言学习规律，做到字、词、句、篇地层层深入，并创设情景，做到词不离句，句不离篇。教师在课堂上要充分使用评价的激励功能，激发学生开口说英语的积极性。

【资料链接】

1.《英语课程标准》(实验稿)，北京师范大学出版社，2001

2. Our fashion show, Book 5, *Primary English for China*

(深圳市南山区蛇口学校　陈辉)

At Home (2)

【设计理念】

1. 拓展学用渠道，开发教学资源。

2. 注重个体差异，点、线、面结合，由浅入深，提供多次的自我展现机会，让学生体验成功的喜悦。

3. 注重过程评价，促进学生发展。

【活动目标】

1. 学生学习有关房间的词汇。

2. 培养学生的观察能力。

3. 学生能理论联系实际，将知识融入生活。

4. 培养学生的英语综合运用能力。

【活动准备】

1. 迪斯尼录像——At Home 的剪辑片断。

2. 多媒体教学课件——幻灯片由教师根据课题制作。

3. 课文的挂图。

4. 自画图——家。

5. 课题歌曲——迪斯尼录像 At Home 的歌曲。

【活动过程】

1. 导入

看录像剪辑片断（Goofy, Mickey and Donald 在不同 rooms 的活动片断），引出课题。

(1) T: Please watch the video with the question "Where are they?"

Video contents: He's in the kitchen. He's at home.
He's in the garden. He's at home.
She is in the bathroom. She's at home.
They're in the bedroom. They're at home.
...

(2) T: Where are they?

(3) Ss: Goofy is in the **kitchen**. He's **at home.**
Mickey is in the **garden**. He's **at home.**

A duck is in the **bathroom**. She's **at home**

Some mice are in the **bedroom**. They are **at home.**

(4) T：Maybe they are mice. Maybe they are squirrels. Anyway，all of them are at ______.

Ss：At home.

2. 看图说话

(1) 演示幻灯片课件，学习一些有关 home 的单词及表达方法。

T：Excellent! Did you preview the text at home?

Ss：Yes!

T：Then what rooms can you hear?

Ss：kitchen，bathroom，bedroom，garden.

T：Good! Today，we'll talk about "home". I'm curious about your home. I want you to talk about your home for us，but first let's revise and learn some words and expressions about home. Look here(Wall picture)：

This is Candy's home. There are four rooms in her home. Do you know what they are?

T：We can cook meals here，so do you know what it is?

Ss：**Kitchen.**

T：What else can we do in the kitchen?

Ss：We can eat meals in the kitchen…

T：Good，where's here?

Ss：**Living room.**

T：What can we do in the living room?

Ss：We can watch TV in the living room.

T：What's the basic form of living?

Ss：live.

T：Good. Look，What is she doing?

Ss：She's having a bath.

T：So，where's here?

Ss：**Bathroom.**

T：Yes，we can have a bath in this room. So we call it a ______

Ss：**Bathroom.**

T：We put some beds in a room，and sleep there. We call the room ______

Ss：**Bedroom.**

T：What else we can do in the bedroom?

Ss：We can do our homework…

T：Can you tell me more rooms and places we learned?

Ss：Classroom / music room / art room…

T：Yes，we can do some things in these places. Now where are you? And what are you doing?

Ss：We are in the classroom. We are studying.

T：Yes，can you talk about Candy's home with your own words now?

(2) 呈现挂图，让学生根据所学知识口头描述挂图。

T：There are four rooms in the picture，they are kitchen，bedroom，bathroom and living room. I like watching TV in the living room. It makes me happy…

Ss：I can see a bathroom. Candy is brushing her hair. I have a bathroom in my home too. I like having a bath in the bathroom. It makes me comfortable…

(让学生自由发挥、扩展)

(3) 呈现幻灯片课件，对所学知识进行适当的延伸。

(隐去主要部分，只提供一些提示图，让学生猜这些人在哪，干什么)

3. 展示作品、简短发言

(1) 老师展示自画图——家。

T：This is my home. There are four rooms. They are kitchen，bedroom，and two living rooms.

(2) 勾勒出自己家的结构布局图。

T：Now I give you some minutes to draw your own home，then I will ask you to talk about your home for us，OK? Begin.

(3) 根据命题，稍做准备后，做简短的发言及描述。

T：Who will be the first one?

S：Me. This is my home. There are four rooms in my home. This is my bedroom. I'm reading books in my bed. This is my bathroom. I have a bath there. It makes me comfortable.

…

(并向全班同学展示自己的作品)

T：All of you did a good job. After class I hope to get more information about your home. Now let's sing a song about our home.

4. 娱乐——歌曲

It's Good to Be at Home

It's good to be at home.

At home.

It's good to be at home.

I love.

You love.

We all love.

It's good to be at home.

【活动评述】

依据新课程标准的精神，我们在教学过程中，从学生生活经验和认知水平出发，科学安排教学内容，合理设计教学任务，运用多种教学手段，开发各种教学资源，借助多媒体教学课件开展形式多样的教学活动，让学生亲身体验、积极参与、共同合作与交流，帮助学生在任务性的教学途径下，发展综合语言运用能力，使学生成为自主学习的主体。

【资料链接】

1. http://www.clipart.com

2. 迪斯尼动画影碟：At Home

（深圳市南山区华侨城小学　陈美贤）

My School

【设计理念】

活动设计力求从学生的学习兴趣，生活经验和认知水平出发，通过体验、实践、参与、合作与交流的学习方式和任务型的教学途径，发展学生的综合语言运用能力，培养学生积极的情感态度及主动思维、大胆实践和自主学习的能力。

【活动目标】

1. 熟练地在不同情景中使用“There be…”的各种句型。例如：

   There's a pencil case in my bag. Are there any books in your bag? …

2. 以小组的形式，创设主题活动，复习旧知，培养学生综合运用语言的能力。
3. 小组自主学习扩展词汇，培养合作精神。

【活动准备】

1. 围绕句型“There is/are…” “Is/Are there…” 组织学生分组讨论，确定活动主题。
2. 组长组织小组成员编写主题剧本，查找词典或使用电脑解决生词问题。
3. 小组学生准备主题卡，并创设情景所需的物品。
4. 教师结合其他教材自制 Welcome to my school 的声像课件(PowerPoint)。
5. 教师自制单词卡：an art room，a library，a dining room，a music room 和 a computer room.
6. 教师准备一个装着有关学习或生活用品的纸袋，并剪好一些小红旗。

【活动过程】

Step 1：Warm-up

1. Sing a song：In My School.

通过歌曲复习“There's a…”和“There are…” 的句型；利用单词卡帮助学生理解 an art room，a library，a dining room，a music room 和 a computer room 等词汇。

2. Ask and answer different questions one by one.

以听促进说，帮助学生克服怕说错或不敢开口说的心理。

Step 2：Lead In

1. Situational talk

   eg 1. Who has got a pencil box?

   2. What's in your box? Is there anything in it?

3. Have you got a pen in your pencil box?

4. Is there a ruler in it?

5. Are there any pens in your pencil box?

6. How many pens are there in it?

7. Can I borrow your pen, please?

创设情景问答,激发学生的学习兴趣。

2. Guessing Games

(1) T: Xiao Zhang has a pencil box on his desk. There are a pen and a pencil in his box. Look! I have a bag on my desk. There's something in it. Let's try to find out what's in it.

eg S1: Is there a ruler in your bag?

T: Yes, there is. You're so clever.

S2: Are there any books?

T: No, there aren't.

...

(2) Let the students do the same games by pair work.

创设轻松、民主、和谐的情景氛围,激发学生积极参与的欲望。

Step 3: Comprehend Anne's school

1. T: Today is Tuesday. Anne's friends Sue and Peter are free. They aren't going to school. They come to Anne's school. Now let's see Anne's school together.

2. Play PowerPoint. Let the students listen to Anne's dialogue twice.

3. Ask the students to answer these questions about Anne's school.

eg (1) What day is today?

(2) What time do Anne's friends go home?

(3) What sport does Peter like?

(4) What's the name of Anne's school?

(5) How many classes does Anne have every day?

(6) How many pupils and teachers are there in Anne's school?

通过观看视听课件播放的声像,回答老师的问题,使学生加深对材料的理解。

4. Let the students watch again.

Step 4: Performance

1. Practice in groups

Divide the class into six groups. Each group takes their things. Get ready to show their performance.

2. Performance and comparison

每个小组轮流展示主题谈话。设小组表演奖,由全班同学共同参与评价。小组准备的主题有: Our classroom, In the street, How about this picture? A big ice-cream shop, Fruit shop 等。

学生在小组活动中提高和发展综合运用语言的能力,形成自主学习的习惯,从而成为课堂的主人并获得学习的成功感。通过竞赛活动，培养了学生的竞赛意识，促进学生的小组合作能力，并让他们学会正确评价他人、赏识别人。

【活动评述】

这节课，教师把"情景，兴趣，活动"与"任务型教学"相结合，从学生的学习生活环境出发创设语境，通过猜游戏、主题表演竞赛等活动，为学生搭建展示的平台，发展了学生英语交际的能力。同时，教师注意在活动中及时进行激励评价，充分调动了学生的学习积极性，并极大地提高了课堂教学效果。

【资料连接】

1.《英语课程标准(实验稿)》，北京师范大学出版社，2001

2. My School, Book 4, *Primary English for China*

(深圳市南山区留仙小学　陈　珍)

Feeling Sick

【设计理念】

本活动采取任务型的教学模式，让学生在教师的指导下，通过感知、体验、实践、参与和合作等方式，实现任务的目标，感受成功。在活动过程中形成积极的学习态度，促进语言实际运用能力的提高。

【活动目标】

通过在教室里创设"医院"这一情景，让学生模拟学习"生病"和"看医生"时的用语，根据教材把这些用语改编成Chant(韵律诗)的形式表演出来。提高学生学习的兴趣和语言表达及语言运用的能力；激发学生参与、探索与创新的信心。

【活动准备】

1. "医生"和"病人"的服装，听诊器，体温表，护士帽。

2. 把教室前半部分简单布置成"医院"。

3. 学生课前先预习课文。

【活动过程】

1. 教师让一学生扮成感冒发烧的样子，学生满面愁容地走进教室。

2. 教师通过询问学生引出"What's the matter (with you)?" 和"What's wrong (with you)?"的句型。通过学生的回答再引出有关生病的句型和词组：I have a headache/have a fever/have a cold/have a stomachache 等。同时，教师立即用电脑播放这些词组，学生进行模仿跟读。

3. 教师引导学生用不同的人称进行提问和回答：What's the matter (wrong) with him/her? He has a cold. She has a fever 等等。学生出于一种真实的交际需要，非常迫切地想说出更多的有关生病的句子，比如：I have a toothache/flu/cough. I feel terrible 等。此时教师应抓住时机进行扩展：I feel horrible/awful. I don't feel well. I've got a pain here. It hurts here. I don't feel like eating 等，同时在屏幕上呈现这些内容。

4. 教师问学生：I have a bad cold. What should I do? 或 What do I need to do?

学生们回答得非常踊跃，给教师许多建议：You should go to hospital/a clinic/see a doctor. You need to take some medicine/have a rest 等。

5. 教师让学生听课文中的Chant，学生跟读并轻轻拍节奏。

6. 学生分六人为一组，根据刚才所听的Chant的内容，进行改编，创作出自己的Chant，并分角色表演。

以下是学生自己改编的韵律诗文：

Tom's Mum：Tom，Tom，what are you doing?
Time for school now.
Quick，quick，quick.

Tom：Mother，mother，I feel sick.
Take me to the doctor.
Quick，quick，quick.

Taxi driver：Today is windy.
Today is cold.
A lot of people want to see a doctor.

Nurse：Hello，hello，I'm a nurse.
I help the doctors
Time and time.

Doctor：Sit down，please.
Are you OK?
What's the matter with you today?
Your face is red.
Your head is hot.
Take some medicine and stay in bed.

7. 教师到各组中指导学生并与之交流，然后根据表演需要把教室的讲台布置成“医院”。每组选出一名评委，组内抽签上台表演，没有表演的同学就拍节奏。最后评出一、二、三等奖，分别给予奖励。

【活动评述】

本活动把枯燥的单词、词组、句型学习变成了生动、活泼的自主学习活动，而且使听说读写的训练紧密结合起来，真正达到了让学生在学中用，在运用中掌握英语的目的；同时也有效地培养了学生运用英语进行交际的能力，充分激发了学生学习语言的兴趣和参与探索与创新的信心。

【资料链接】

1.《英语课程标准(实验稿)》，北京示范大学出版社，2001

2. 黄爱玲、齐捷锋，《课堂教学情境创设》，中小学英语教学与研究，2003 年第 7 期

3. Feeling sick，Book 8，*Primary English for China*

（深圳市南山实验学校　段　群）

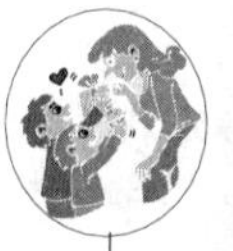

Helping at Home (1)

【设计理念】

教师应该为学生提供自主学习和相互交流的机会以及充分表现和自我发展的空间，创造条件让学生能够探究自己感兴趣的问题并进行自主解决。我们主张通过体验、实践、讨论、合作、探究等方式，发展学生听、说的综合语言技能。

【活动目标】

1. 让学生掌握句型：How do you help at home? I always(usually/sometimes/never)… How does your dad (mum/brother/sister/grandpa/grandma) help at home? He/She always (usually/sometimes/never)…

2. 会说自己在家中所做的一些家务事，并会把他们运用到实际生活当中。

【活动准备】

1. 教师准备关于拖把、扫把、抹布、洗洁净、撒水壶、水盆、餐具等这些东西的图片。

2. 学生自己画的自己家从周一至周日所做的家务事的表格。

3. 教师准备好电脑、课件、磁带、录音机等。

【活动过程】

1. 看电脑学习句型。先认真仔细听和跟读 Pat 和 Tim 的对话，然后根据图中所示 Pat 家的家务劳动表格，让学生回答下列问题：How does Pat help at home? How does Pat's dad/mum help at home?

2. 给学生发一张调查表，让他们根据自己在家的表现，完成表格。要求使用句型 How do you help at home? 最好能用上 always，sometimes，often，usually，never 这些词。

How do you help at home?

	Wash the dishes	Sweep the floor	Water the plants	Make the bed	Clean a room	Set the table
Monday						
Tuesday						
Wednesday						
Thursday						
Friday						
Saturday						
Sunday						

3. 实际操练。让学生每四人一组用自己的表格来进行讨论：How do you help at home? How does your dad help at home? How does your mum help at home?

4. 鼓励学生提问。有一名学生大声问我："How do you help at home, Miss Feng?"听到这个问题，我非常欣慰：我们的学生会反问老师问题了。我自豪地回答："I always cook. I usually wash the dishes. I sometimes sweep the floor. I never water the plants."我的话音刚落，班上又一个同学接着问："How does your husband help at home?" 我看着学生期盼的眼神，明白同学们都关心老师，更关注老师的家庭生活，所以我又回答："He is very busy, so he always waters the plants. He sometimes makes his bed. He never sweeps the floor. He never washes the dishes. He never cleans the rooms. He never…"这时，又有学生接着问：How does your son help at home? 全班学生听后都会心地大笑起来。班上的气氛非常活跃。我也开朗起来，调皮地答道："He always sweeps the floor. He usually makes his bed. He sometimes sets the table. He never cleans the rooms."

5. 因势利导，鼓励学生说话。我的回答引起了学生的兴趣，我乘机转换说话对象。我说："Now I want you to tell me Something. How does your dad/mum/brother/sister help at home?" 学生们都争先恐后，大声地说："My mum always washes the dishes. She always cleans the rooms. She usually washes the clothes. But my dad never sweeps the floor at home. He never washes the dishes. He never makes his bed. He never… He never helps at home." 这时候，小组讨论变成了全班的辩论。有的同学说妈妈辛苦，包揽了家中所有的家务；有的说爸爸勤劳，要拼命赚钱养家。同学们争执不休，各抒己见。同学们都看着我，于是我总结道："Dad and Mum work hard for us. We love our Dad and Mum. We should always help at home." 同学们都扬手说："OK!"

【活动评述】

学生根据情景，大胆创新，展开辩论，使整节课既做到学用结合，又做到寓思想教育于语言教学之中。

【资料链接】

1. 章兼中，《小学英语教育学》，山西高校联合出版社，1996

2. 《英语课程标准（实验稿）》，北京师范大学出版社，2001

3. Helping at home, Book 6, *Primary English for China*

（深圳市南山区前海小学　冯永勤）

On the Farm（2）

【设计理念】

以认知心理学为指导，突出认知、情感、智力三方面的教学特征。采取形式多样的课堂活动，利用多媒体提供比课本更生动、更真实的情景，使学生获取、处理和使用信息，让学生在听、说、唱的游戏中，有意无意地吸取信息、活跃思维、掌握技能，达到语言实践的目的。

【活动目标】

1．帮助学生借助多媒体、图片、单词卡等形式，学会 horse、cow、duck、chicken、pig、sheep 几个词汇，并用"There is(are)…"句型表达。

2．培养学生良好的英语学习习惯，让学生热爱动物和大自然。

3．通过多媒体教学培养学生观察事物的能力。

【活动准备】

有关动物的头饰、图片、多媒体课件、生词卡片等。

【活动过程】

Step 1：Warm-up

1．唱歌曲 Old MacDonald Has a Farm，边唱边做动作，渲染轻松愉快的英语氛围。

2．用电脑呈现已学过的动物名称，即复习旧课，又激起学习新课的情绪。

Step 2：Lead In

1．呈现 Welcome to our farm 的图片及六个有关动物的单词，先让学生对学习的内容有初步的了解。

2．展示动物并逐一将图片、单词卡贴在墙上，反复进行朗读，让学生从无声学习到有声学习，加深对内容的印象。

3．用各种形式操练单词，重点区分个别相似单词，如 horse 与 house 的发音。

4．听声音分辨动物：荧屏出现新学的六个动物的单词，老师选择其中一种动物，动物发出声音，学生说出动物的英语名称。

5．游戏(猜动物)：荧屏上出现动物身体的一部分，学生判断是什么动物。要求先说出动物的名称，再用"There is(are)…"句型去表示。

Step 3：What's Missing?

将学生分成四人一小组，教师在组内摆放动物图片，学生进行观察，由一位学生闭眼抽出其中一张，争眼后回忆并说出“消失”的图片上的动物的名称。

Step 4：Drawing

学生准备好纸和铅笔，根据老师念的一段描述农场的话，进行想像作画。看哪位学生画得最适合老师的短文意思，教师将返位学生的画呈现在黑板上，再让这位学生用自己的语言描述自己的画。

Step 5：Guessing Game

1. 说明活动的操作规程：教师(或一学生)出示一些动物的单词卡片，让另一位学生从老师手中抽取一张单词卡片(不许看卡片)，再请其他学生就卡片内容向老师进行提问(问题必须是一般疑问句)。老师将根据卡片内容进行 Yes/No 的回答，学生根据老师的回答进行猜测。

例如：抽出的卡片是 horse，其他学生可以这么问：Is it big? Is it tall? Has it got long ears? Has it got short legs? 教师根据实际情况做 yes/no 的回答。一般情况下，当问到最后几个问题时，学生就能猜出来了。

2. 请一两位学生上来当小老师做示范，其他学生向他提问，教师也可参与提问，以便让学生更明白游戏的操作方法。

3. 将学生分成小组，分发小卡片给每个小组之后，便开展小组活动。

这种活动能发挥学生的主观能动性。学生根据所提供的信息回忆所有与之有关的单词，并快速做出反应，从而促进了知识的滚动和复习，培养了记忆力、想像力，发散思维及小组合作的能力。

Step 6：Miming the Animals

让学生分别带上各种动物的头饰，边说边做该动物特征的动作。要求用上所学动物名称和 There be 句型。让学生伸展手脚，调节较长时间的坐姿，用相应的身体语言，把枯燥无味的语言变为有趣、活泼的全身心模仿。这样下来，身体语言配合口头语言，更加深学生对所学的知识的印象。

【活动评述】

本课的教学目标明确。通过多媒体的应用和各种教学活动，加强了学生的听说训练，充分调动了学生的学习积极性，发挥了学生的学习主动性。在语言的实践中，学生们的胆量、应变、合作的意识也在不知不觉中得到了锻炼，这充分体现了面向全体学生、以学生为主体的教学观念。

【资料链接】

1. 《小学教学全书——英语卷》，上海教育出版社，1999

2. 罗丹，《小学综合英语教师手册》，中山大学出版社，2002

3. On the farm, Book 4, *Primary English for China*

(深圳市南山区南头城小学　付晓霞)

In My Neighborhood

【设计理念】

力求创设真实有趣的英语情景，通过生动活泼的英语活动，让学生在活动中学会语言知识，体会英语乐趣，激发创新思维，热爱英语课堂，从而真正达到提高课堂效率，实施素质教育的目的。

【活动目标】

1. 学生掌握描述社区以及社区里的设施方位等的英语单词、句型。

2. 学生能够用英语描述自己的社区。

【活动准备】

学生事先拍好的照片或画好的一些社区设施图片，录音机，幻灯片。

【活动过程】

Step 1：Warm-up

(Say the rhythm and do some actions)

Pick up, put down

Stand up, stand up

Clap left clap right

Clap up clap down

Look up look down

Turn around, sit down

Step 2：Lead In

T：We do morning exercises every day, and we usually do in our school playground. But sometimes I do my exercise in my neighborhood. Look! This is my neighborhood.

(The teacher takes out a picture of the neighborhood and say: Let's talk about it)

Step 3：Learn New Words and New Sentences

T：What's in the neighborhood?

(The teacher helps the students answer)

Ss：There are many buildings.

T：Yes. Good. Look. I live in Building A. There is a lift in Building A.

(Point to the picture of a lift and make the students understand the meaning of lift)

T: Let's read the word together.

(The pupils read the words twice)

T: Where is the lift?

(Help the pupils say: It's in the building)

(Teach the preposition: in)

The same way to teach the new words: balcony, tennis court, a fishpond, a garden and a clubhouse.

The same way to review the prepositions: on, beside, in the center of, behind and near.

Step 4: Listen and Answer

Let the students listen to the tape twice and answer the following questions:

1. What's in the neighborhood?

2. What do I do in the neighborhood?

Step 5: Design Their Favorite Neighborhood

Ask the students to take out the pictures they have prepared and design a neighborhood. The students make dialogues like this:

S1: What's in our neighborhood?

S2: There is a lift. There is also a clubhouse. There is a garden, too.

S3: Is there a fishpond?

S4: Yes.

S5: Where is it?

S6: It's near the clubhouse.

S7: We should have a swimming pool near the garden.

S8: I don't think so. I think we should have the swimming pool in the clubhouse.

Step 6: An Action

The designers come to the front to introduce their neighborhood. The other students can ask some questions about the neighborhood.

The designers offer the price of the building in their neighborhood and the other students decide how much they will buy.

eg Designer: Look! This is the best neighborhood. There is a tennis court. There is a clubhouse. There are also many trees and beautiful flowers in the neighborhood. There are also big and comfortable balconies.

The other students may ask: Is there a swimming pool? Where is it? Is there a lift? Where is it? etc.

The designer must answer the questions and persuade the students to buy.

Step 7: An Interview

Ask the students to go around the classroom to interview the buyers.

eg S1：Why did you buy this building?

S2：Because there is a big clubhouse in the neighborhood. I like to play in the clubhouse. There are many trees. The air will be very good. So I buy this building.

【活动评述】

这堂课围绕社区这个话题设计了三个贴近学生生活的活动。活动过程比较注重学生的学习兴趣的培养和提高，使得单词和句型的教学不再那么枯燥。整节课活动量大，学生参与性很强，突出了学生在课堂上的主体地位。

【资料链接】

《英语课程标准(实验稿)》，北京师范大学出版社，2001

（深圳市南山区华侨城小学　周丽仙）

Clothes

【设计理念】

按照英语课程标准提出的“采用活动途径，倡导体验参与”精神，通过听、说、读、写、游、玩、做等各种教学活动，让学生从具体而生动的亲身体验中逐步掌握语言基本技能，提高实际运用语言的能力。

【活动目标】

1. 能够在完成语言活动的过程中使用“This be…”句型描述自己或他人的衣服。

2. 能听懂或发出与衣服相关的指令，如：Put on a shirt. Take off your shoes.

3. 会唱歌曲 My Clothes。

4. 能得体地穿衣，并具有初步的审美能力。

【活动准备】

1. 学生每人自制一套衣服单词小卡片。

2. 老师准备一批衣服、课件、flashcards。

【活动过程】

1. 课前热身

(1) 师生同唱一首英文歌：Who is Wearing Yellow Today?

(2) T：Who is wearing a shirt/a dress/a T-shirt/shorts/trousers today?

Ss：(穿着相关衣服的学生可以自由回答)I am.

2. 穿衣比赛

每次由四个学生上台比赛。参赛学生根据老师(或者另一个学生)发出的不同的命令(如：Put on a T-shirt/a jacket/a shirt/shorts/trousers/shoes/；Take off your shirt/your shoes/your hat)，做相应的动作，动作正确的可为本组赢得一分。

3. 新课导入

(1) 老师手持一张单词卡片，卡片上有一双袜子，老师用手或白纸遮住其中一只，引导学生回答：“What's this?” “This is a sock.”

再展示一双袜子的完整图片，引导学生回答："What are they?" "These are socks."

(2) 学生试着找规律，区别句型"This is…" 和"These are…" 的用法。

(3) 老师手持多张衣服单词卡片，学生分组练习"This is…"/"These are…" 句型。

4. Fashion Show

随着节奏明快的音乐，学生纷纷到讲台前面走一段台步，并用刚学的句子描述自己的衣服：This is my shirt. It is yellow. These are my shoes. They are blue. They are nice.

5. 学唱英文歌 My Clothes

This is my cap here. This is my shirt here.

This is my skirt here that I like to wear.

These are my socks here. These are my shoes here.

These are my jeans here that I like to wear.

(鼓励学生把歌词里的"This is…" 和"These are…" 改成"That is…" 和"Those are…")

7. 游戏 Dress：帮小猴穿衣服

这是一个网上游戏，请学生独自上台操作，根据电脑语音提示把相应的服饰放在小猴相对照的地方，正确者可得一分。例如：Please give me shirt. Please give me my hat.

如果网络条件不许可，老师可以让学生带布娃娃到课堂上，由老师或学生发出穿衣的指令，其他学生给布娃娃穿上相应的衣服。

8. Homework

(1) 向朋友和家长描述自己身上的衣服。

(2) 在纸上设计自己喜欢的衣服，并涂上颜色。

【活动评述】

本课在教学过程中，按照新课标提出的"采用活动途径，倡导体验参与"的精神，以活动为核心组织教学，使学习和活动有机地结合起来，以"动"促学，以"动"促用，让学生在活动中学会英语，并用英语进行交际。

【资料链接】

1. 九年义务教育小学教科书

2. 北京新知堂少儿英语网

(深圳市南山区华侨城小学　钟美莹)

Our Fashion Show (2)

【设计理念】

一堂有趣的口语活动交际课，使孩子们都积极参与到课堂教学活动中来，让孩子们在轻松、愉快的环境中学习语言知识。活动通过一场服装秀来激发孩子们的表现欲和正确的审美观。

【活动目标】

1. 能熟练地说出各种服装的名称。

2. 能根据天气变化自己选择衣服。

3. 能说出人们的不同穿着。

【活动准备】

一年四季穿的各种服饰、给模特编号的彩色号码卡片、生词闪视卡及服装变化的各种动画课件。

【活动过程】

1. 找颜色——教师说一个颜色单词，学生找到带有这种颜色的事物，并说出带有颜色的句型：It's blue. It's red…

2. 找服装——教师说一个服装单词，穿着这种服装的学生站起来，指着自己的衣服并说出它的名字：jacket，jeans…

3. 练句型1，说出双方相对应的服装。老师描述衣服，学生描述衣服；老师描述裤子，学生描述裤子。

T：I am wearing blue jeans.

Ss：I am wearing red jeans.

T：I am wearing a white shirt.

Ss：I am wearing a blue shirt.

4. 练句型2，互相说出对方的服装。老师描述学生的服装，学生描述老师的服装。

T：You are wearing a yellow jacket.

Ss：You are wearing a blue shirt.

T：You are wearing blue pants.

Ss：You are wearing blue jeans.

T：You are wearing white shoes.

Ss：You are wearing brown shoes.

然后，同桌分小组进行对话。

S1：You are wearing a red sweater.

S2：You are wearing a orange sweater.

5. 利用带到教室来的实物，复习表示服装的单词。然后，教师做出在不同天气下的反应，让学生为自己挑选服装。

T：I am very cold.（装出很冷的样子）

Ss：Put on your coat and scarf.（找到大衣和围巾并递给老师）

T：I am very hot.（装出很热的样子）

Ss：Put on your shirt and shorts.（找到衬衫和短裤并递给老师）

然后，让几对学生上台进行表演。

6. 听音，给课件中的卡通人物穿上服装。学生根据老师的描述，给屏幕上的人物配上正确的服装。

T：She is wearing a purple skirt.

Ss：Move the purple skirt to the little girl.（把紫色毛衣拖到小女孩身上）

T：She is wearing brown pants.

Ss：Move the brown pants to the little girl.（把棕色裤子拖到小女孩身上）

7. 猜谜语：老师说出班上某个同学的穿着，让其他同学猜猜他是谁。

T：This is a boy. He is wearing a blue jacket，grey pants and brown shoes. Who is he?

S1：He is Li Ming.

T：No，he isn't.

S2：Is he Liu Jun?

T：Yes，he is.

然后，学生做小组活动，猜对方是谁。

S3：She is wearing a pink dress，white socks and red shoes.

S4：She is Jane.

8. 给几个学生发号码牌，鼓励他们在前台走模特步，并摆出一个造型。让其他的学生做观众说出台上模特的穿着。

S5：Number 1 is wearing a red dress and pink shoes.

S6：Number 2 is wearing a blue hat，purple sweater and black pants.

【活动评述】

本节课中时装秀的主题与孩子们的生活联系较紧密。我们通过以上的这些口语交际活动不仅能让孩子们认识日常生活中的服装，还能让孩子们描述出人们的不同穿着；同时，也培养了孩子们对穿着的审美观和自理能力。

【资料链接】

1. 北京新知堂少儿英语教育网

2. Our fashion show，Book 5，*Primary English for China*

（深圳市南山区前海小学　黄光宗）

Preposition

【设计理念】

依据新课标英语教学的基本原则，我们设计了方位介词的教学活动，意在提高学生英语知识，促进听力习惯的养成，激发学习的兴趣，培养团队合作精神和创新意识。

【活动目标】

1. 学习和巩固有关交通工具、家禽、水果、玩具等的单词。
2. 会简单描述一幅图，会靠听力获取信息并会画下来所听到的内容。
3. 培养学生团队合作的精神。

【活动准备】

1. 老师准备三幅图。
2. 学生准备一张白纸和一支笔。

【活动过程】

1. 整个班(四十五人)分成九组，每组五人，五人中又把两人与另外三人分开相对而坐。这样整个班的桌椅摆放如下图：

2. 每组的三个人取出纸和笔，做好画画的准备。老师取出已绘好的三张图，这三张图上画有交通工具、家禽、水果、玩具等，每一张图都会比上张多一些东西，而这些东西的英文名字都是孩子们学过的。三张图如下所示：

图 1

图 2

图 3

3. 老师手里举着第一张图，站到右边，面对每组的那两个孩子，在每组三个孩子的背后，站一分钟。对面的两个孩子轻声描述他们所看到的图，其他三人则迅速画下他们所听到的内容。其他组的同学不能偷听或偷看图。

学生看着第一张图可以说的内容为：

A boy is on the grasses. A girl is on the grasses, too. A dog is on the grasses. A table is on the grasses. A pizza is on the table. A banana is on the table. A flower is under a tree. A ball is in the toy box. A plane is in the sky. A ship is in the sea. A truck is on the road. Three students are in the train.

4. 老师依次从第一组走到第九组，在每一组的面前待一分种。老师手里一直拿着同一幅图。前面几组已经看到了图的同学可以通过回忆继续向他们的另三个同组成员描述画的内容。

5. 老师举着第一幅图从第一组走到第九组后，再拿第二幅图走一次，最后拿着第三幅图走一次。这样，每个画画的同学手里都画有一幅图，但大家的图肯定会不一样。

学生看着第二幅图增加说的内容为：

A car is on the road. A sheep is on the grasses. A cat is under the tree. A chicken is on the grasses. A flower is on the grasses. Two ducks are on the pool.

学生看着第三幅图增加说的内容为：

A school bus is on the road. A horse is on the grasses. It is behind the boy and the girl. A giraffe is on the grasses. A chicken is under the giraffe.

6. 把每个同学画的图展示出来，并请他们描述自己画的画。最后再呈现老师的第三幅图，评选出最佳合作小组。

【活动评述】

学生们为了画出更多的内容，必须认真听组内成员说，这样就有利于提高他们的英语听的能力。这个活动也提高了学生们的绘画能力，还促进了他们团结合作的精神及学习英语的兴趣。

【资料链接】

Toys, Book 2, *Primary English for China*

（深圳市南山区南油小学　黄　欣）

Toys

【设计理念】

在分析小学低年级孩子的生理、心理特征的基础上，从学生的兴趣、生活经验和认知水平出发，在教学过程中积极探索任务型教学途径，创造性地设计贴近学生生活的教学活动，以吸引和组织学生在课堂上积极地思考、交流和合作，使学生在视听、说唱、玩做中轻松、愉快地完成学习任务，从而努力做到"为用而学、在用中学、学以致用"，真正使"课堂活动化，活动交际化"。

【活动目标】

1. 认知目标

(1) 能听懂并会说本课要求的玩具名称，如：car，bus，ball，boat，ship，balloon，doll 等。

(2) 会应用本课句型进行问与答的对话与交流，如：

Is it a…

Yes，it is a…

No，it is not a…

2. 情感目标

通过创设"送生日礼物"的情景，对学生进行情感教育，让他们学会关爱他人。

3. 能力目标

(1) 通过以猜字为特点的系列课堂活动，使学生在真实的情景中运用所学的语言知识，做到学有所用。

(2) 通过围绕主题 Toys 的小组活动及自制神奇玩具等活动，培养学生的语言综合运用能力和创新能力。

【活动准备】

1. 教师准备小汽车纸板教具、玩具图片字卡、装有各种玩具的纸箱一个、小礼物一份、多媒体课件等。

2. 学生准备正方形白纸一张、铅笔一枝、彩色笔四枝。

【活动过程】

Step 1：Lead In

1. 课前热身

师生共同演唱英文歌曲 Roll That Ball(其内容与玩具有关)。

2. 每日说话：姓名故事

师：今天我们要说一个男孩的姓名故事，在他的名字里有一个玩具汽车，猜猜看，他是谁？

生：He is Care.

师：现在咱们来听一听 Care 的姓名故事吧。

给出四个以其名字开头的英语单词，然后把这些词串起来，编成一个小故事。如：c→cup，a→apple，r→red，e→egg。

Hello，I am care. I am six years old. This is a cup. It is red. I drink water with it. I like eating apples and eggs. They are good. That's all，thank you.

师：根据学生的姓名故事提 1～2 个问题，旨在检查其余学生听的情况。

3. 引出课题

教师把小汽车纸板教具的背面展示给学生，让他们猜是什么。

学生：It is a car.

教师把写有 Toys 的小汽车纸板教具贴在黑板上。

学生跟读标题。

Step 2：Language Learning

1. 学习玩具名称

师：这辆小汽车里装满了玩具，我们借助图片字卡来教玩具词。

2. 学说话

师：你们喜欢什么玩具？

生：我喜欢……

生：我喜欢……

3. 学习新句型

师：车里的玩具都是 Alice 的家人送给她的，因为明天是她的生日（教师从学生情况一览表中获得此信息）。想知道都是些什么玩具吗？

师：Is it a car?（摇头）

No，it is not a car.（自问自答）

Is it a ball?

Yes，it is a ball.（点头，回答）

学生跟着老师重复问句与答句数遍。

4. 语言实践

师生问答、生生问答（借助实物或图片）。

Step 3：Consolidation

师：（A guessing game）猜一猜这些是不是 Alice 的爷爷、奶奶、爸爸、妈妈、叔叔、婶婶、哥哥、姐姐送的礼物。

（利用多媒体课件）游戏规则：请猜"Yes"的学生出示食指和中指，做"V"字状，并作答："Yes，it is a…" 猜"No"的学生，出示食指，做"I"字状，并作答："No，it is not a…"

屏幕上：Is it a car?

Ss：Yes，it is a car.

Ss：No，it is not a car.

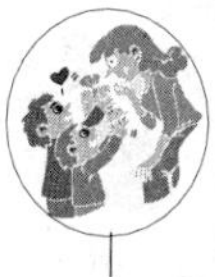

教师按键，显示画面和答案，判出胜方。

（通过这种师生互动的游戏来巩固所学知识）

Step 4：Extended Activities

1. 问话猜

师：老师也有一件礼物送给 Alice，请用句型“Is it a…” 猜猜看是什么？

生：Is it a car/ bus / toy rabbit?

师：Yes，it is a toy rabbit. It is white. It is small，but it is lovely.

（示范描述玩具，为后面的活动做铺垫）

学生向 Alice 投去羡慕的眼光。

师：你们别失望，老师也有礼物送给你们，它们在这个箱子里。

2. 唱歌猜

全班分成四个组，用唱歌的方式猜箱子里的玩具，被猜中的玩具属于猜中的组，活动直至四个组都有一个玩具为止。

Ss：What's in the box?

What's in the box?

Can you guess?

What's in the box?

Group 1：Is it a doll?

Group 2：Is it a car?

师：Yes，it is a car.

于是，小汽车属于 Group 2，以此类推，活动继续进行，直到每个组都有一个玩具。

3. 小组活动

教师把学生分成四组，围成四个圆圈，每组讨论及描述各自的玩具。

最后由组长汇报讨论的结果。

Step 5：Language Production

1. 展示自制玩具

师：同学们，我这里有一个神奇的玩具，它的神奇就在于能满足你们想要玩具的愿望。但在得到玩具之前，你们必须要闯关，先回答两个问题：What color do you like? What number do you like? 回答完后，你们就能得到想要的玩具了。

师：What color do you like，Tim?

Tim：I like yellow.

师：What number do you like?

Tim：I like number three.

师：Count three. It is a car.

喜欢这个玩具吗？下面我就教你们怎样制作这个神奇的玩具。

2. 制作方法

(1) 拿起桌面上正方形的纸，向着中心对折四个三角形。

(2) 翻面，用同样的方法重复刚才的步骤。

(3) 向内写出八种玩具的名称，向外用四种彩色笔写出对应的颜色词。

（4）找自己的同伴或好友，按先前老师的示范，分享神奇的玩具。

自制玩具平面图：

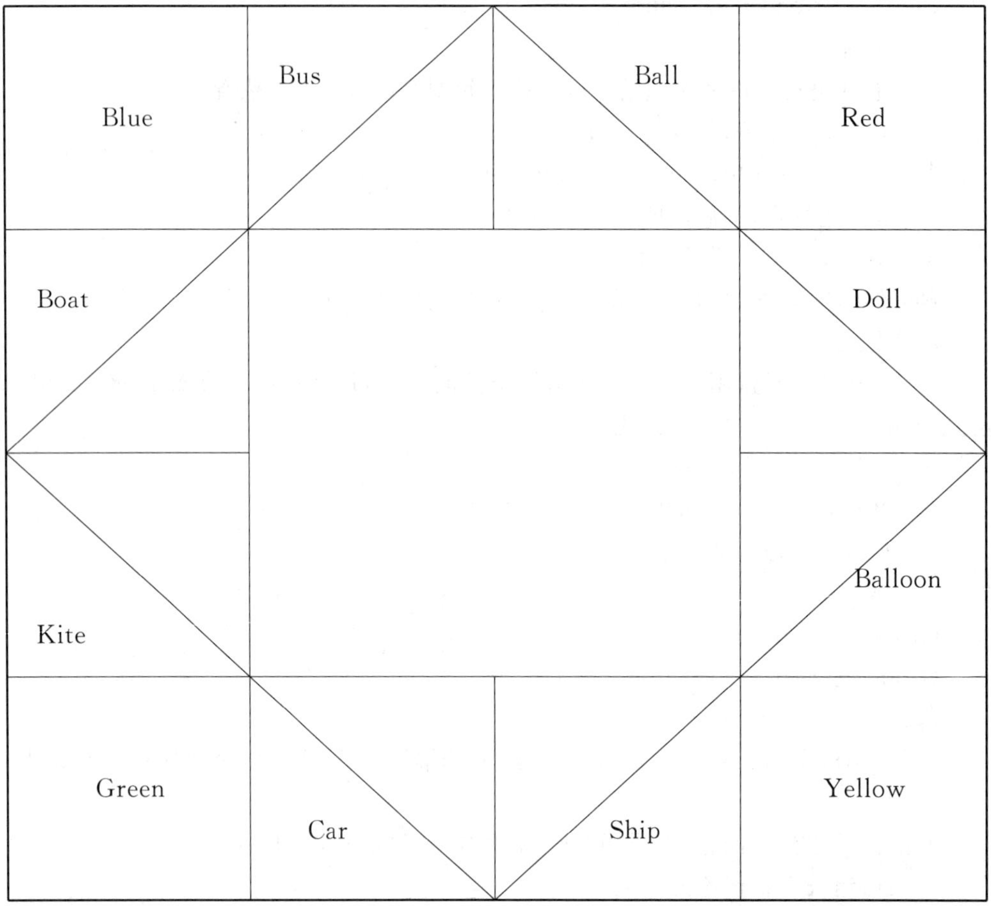

【活动评述】

1. 巧妙导入，激发兴趣。利用学生 Care 的名字引出姓名故事，再用自制并写有"Toys"字样的小汽车纸板教具引出课题。

2. "猜"字贯穿始终，学生情绪保持高涨。笔者整堂课抓住一个"猜"字，以"送生日礼物"为主线，用形式多样的课堂活动（如判断猜、说话猜、唱歌猜等）来传授新知，巩固新知，学生自始至终保持积极主动的学习状态。

3. 学生的创造性劳动：自制神奇玩具。这个环节把教学推向高潮。要制作的玩具对学生来说并不陌生，其实就是他们常玩的"东、南、西、北"。笔者在原来的基础上，改变了一下传统的做法和玩法，把所学的知识（如颜色、数字和玩具名称等）融进了游戏中，使学习任务变得易学、易做、易掌握，学生也感到其乐无穷。

【资料链接】

北京新知堂网站（www. xizhitang. com）

（深圳市南山外国语学校教师　金有选）

Fun with Shapes

【设计理念】

结合学生所学过的“I can see a / two…” 及“There is / There are…”句型，利用游戏帮助他们学习表示形状的新单词。利用学生玩的穿绳游戏来学习各种形状，教师操作起来很方便，学生学起来也感觉亲切。

【活动目标】

1. 学习 shape，circle，triangle，square 等表示形状的新单词。

2. 复习“I can see a / two…”“There is / There are…”句型。

3. 学习表示颜色的词。

【活动准备】

单词卡、用彩纸剪的各种形状及彩色的包装绳(各同学自备，绳子的颜色自定，但是绳子不能太长，要确保打结后手可以撑起来)。

【活动过程】

Step 1：Warm-up

Sing a song Color Song

通过歌曲的演唱，营造愉悦的学习气氛，激发学生的兴趣，让学生在无意之中就复习了表示颜色的词。

Step 2：Presentation

T(hold out two hands and ask)：What's in my hand?

T：Look! It's a line. What shape is it? It's a line.

What color is it? It's red.

Now. Let me combine these two ends. What can I make with the line?

What shape is it? It's a rectangle. What color is it? It's…

What else can I make? I can make a triangle.

What color is it? It's yellow. We can see a yellow triangle.

T：Is it a triangle? No, it is a square.

How many squares can you see? I can see one.

I can see a blue square.

Now, there is a blue circle in my hand…

利用猜的游戏呈现新课，极大地调动了学生的积极性。学生绞尽脑汁想猜出老师手里的东西，这充分发挥了他们的想像力。教师出示绳子以后，把两头接上，用手把绳子撑开，就可以形成各种形状，这样让学生学起新单词来也比较直观。

Step 3：Practice

1. Listen to the tape.

2. Read all the new words together. Then check several pupils to see whether they have learned all the new words or not.

Step 4：Listen and Do

1. Show me your line.
2. Combine two ends together.
3. Make a circle.
4. Make a square.
5. Make a triangle
6. Make a star.

The first time, the teacher makes shapes with the pupils together while giving the orders.

The second time, the teacher just gives orders without doing anything in order to check whether the pupils can make the correct shapes, but the pupils should repeat what the teacher said.

The third time, the teacher asks several pupils who have the lines with the same color to come to the front and stand in line, and chooses one other pupil to give the orders.

Then the teacher guides the pupils to say:

I can see four circles. They are green. There are four green circles.

在“听和做”的活动中，老师第一次边发指令边做动作，是为了帮助学生巩固所学的新单词；第二次老师只说不做是为了检查学生是否能听明白指令，及是否能做出正确的反应；而学生重复老师的话，是为下一个活动做准备；第三次是为了让学生能更多地亲身参与活动，并在老师的引导下使用需要掌握的句型。因为课前同学们都准备了绳子，所以每个学生都能参加到活动中来。

Step 5：Group Work

The group leader gives the orders and the other students make shapes.

培养学生合作学习的精神及在实践中运用语言的能力。

【活动评述】

这是一个结合句型教学来学习新单词的活动。把单词的教学和学生玩的穿绳游戏联系在一起，使所学知识和现实生活有效地结合起来，让学生在愉快的气氛中学习，真正实现寓教于乐。

【资料链接】

1.《英语课程标准(实验稿)》，北京师范大学出版社，2001

2. Fun with shapes, Book 5, *Primary English for China*

（深圳市南山区学府小学　蓝文苑）

My Room

【设计理念】

通过活动和表演，给学生创造充分的学习空间，培养学生的英语交流能力，提高学生的口语水平，让学生通过合作来体验语言、体验生活、体验学习的过程与快乐。活动把语言训练与学生的实际生活相结合，体现“在学中用，在用中学”的新的教学思想与理念。

【活动目标】

1. 知识目标

（1）巩固操练“There is/are…” 句型。

（2）能在特定情景中熟练运用“I like…”和“What colour is/are the…”句型。

2. 能力目标

（1）培养学生的观察与分析能力。

（2）培养学生的交际能力和创造能力，发展学生的个性。

（3）拓宽学生的知识面，提高学生的综合素质。

3. 情感目标

（1）激发学生学习的参与意识、综合运用知识的意识、团结合作意识和审美情趣。

（2）激发学生学习英语的兴趣，提高学习积极性。

（3）培养学生爱家庭、爱家乡的美好情感。

【活动准备】

1. 各种家具图片，钥匙模型，小区居住图。

2. 观察、设计、想像自己可爱的家。

【活动过程】

Step 1：Warm-up

1. 教师示范：Take a paper→Fold the paper→Draw a house→Cut the paper→Show a house.

2. T：Whose house is this? (It's Pat's)

Step 2：Lead In

1. 师：Pat 的房子里空空的，让我们去家具店为她挑选一些家具，好吗？

2. Act out the dialogues：Shopping.

(desk, bed, sofa, chair, table, wardrobe, shelf, curtains, wall…)

3. 帮老师装饰新家：There is a…

T：I have a new house. Can you help me to put some furniture in my home?

(Ask pupils to put some pictures in the room)

4. Talk about the room.

Step 3：Practive

布置自己的家：

1. 剪好房子，再画家具(六人一组活动)。

2. 添加些其他的摆设：TV, flower, picture, lamp, radio, vase…

3. Pair work：Ask and answer.

Step 4：Feed back

请到我家来做客：

1. 简单描绘居住的小区环境。

2. Act out the dialogues：A Visit to…

3. 游戏：和老师做邻居。模拟搬到X小区，用英语介绍自己的新家，并取走钥匙。

【活动评述】

本设计以活动为核心组织教学，使学习和活动完美有机地结合。学生通过折纸、剪纸、绘画、买家具、搬家具等各种与生活实际密切相关的活动，除了能学会一些生活小常识外，还能充分发挥想像力、拓宽思维，在活动中发现自身的价值，发挥自己的特长。这些活动使学生都想说和有话可说，以“动”促说，以“动”促用，把英语从学生嘴里“逼”出来。

【资料链接】

1. http：//www.pep.com.cn

2. My room, Book 4, *Primary English for China*

(深圳市南山区南山小学　劳静仪)

On the Farm (3)

【设计理念】

整个教学活动的设计，坚持情感目标与英语学习相结合；坚持多媒体与教材相结合，突破重难点，力求手段创新；坚持“以教师为主导，学生为主体，活动为主线”的思路；坚持活化教材，大力开发课程资源，拓展学用渠道。

【活动目标】

1. 从学生的情感入手，让学生了解动物的习性，了解动物对人类的用处。

2. 熟练掌握句型：What's your favourite animal? I like ducks…

【活动准备】

准备一块小黑板，黑板上画上动物、动物喜欢的食物以及这些食物的用处。

【活动过程】

Step 1：Warming-up

1. Sing an English song Old McDonlad Has a Farm.

2. Greeting.

3. Say all kinds of the animals.

4. Write down the animal words on the blackboard.

本环节通过演唱歌曲，创设了学习语言的良好氛围。学生随着欢快的音乐，很快进入学习的状态。

Step 2：Presentation

1. 引导学生看黑板，让学生仔细观察，初步感知并认读动物单词，如：snake, elephant, dog, cat, monkey, pig, sheep, rabbit, fish 等。

2. 用红笔圈出在农场里的动物，如：pig, chicken, sheep, horse, cow, duck。

3. 教师出示教学卡片，将教学卡片与单词相结合，使学生快速记忆农场里的动物单词。

T：What's this?

Ss：It's a duck/a horse/a pig/a chicken/a sheep/a cow.

4. 以 4 人小组为单位，通过问与答的形式操练这些单词。

5. 上网 http://www.bbc.com→children's→games→come outside game.

利用局域网，把学生带到牛场、鸡屋去参观。学生通过漂亮而又动感的画面，了解到牛可以为我们提供牛奶，母鸡可以为我们提供鸡蛋，公鸡可以为我们打鸣。

6. 教师在黑板上示范板书：What's your favourite animal?

I like ducks.

教师边写边读，写完后学生齐读。

Step 3：Practice

1. 教师在一块小黑板上，画了其他的一些动物，让同学们说一说它们的用处。从学生认识动物入手，让学生了解更多动物的用处。比如，小狗是我们的朋友，可以帮助我们看家；我们的羊毛衫来自羊毛。

2. 在认识了动物对人类的用处后，学生做连线练习。

S1：The dog can look after our house.

S2：The hen can give us the egg.

S3：The cow can give us the milk.

3. 问与答：学生在了解了动物的习性与用处后，才能真实地表达他们的情感。

S1：What's your favourite animal?

S2：I like cows…

4. 发给每个学生一张调查表，让他们根据表里的内容，调查同学们最喜欢的动物是什么。学生在调查的过程中，能运用所学知识，并且学会与人交往。同时，还能将英语与数学学科进行整合。

Name	What's your favourite animal?

Step 4：Assessment

课堂上的各种练习，教师以小组的形式给以评价。评价时给的都是小圆片，其中孕育着 farm 这个单词。但教师直到课的结束，才将小圆片连接起来。

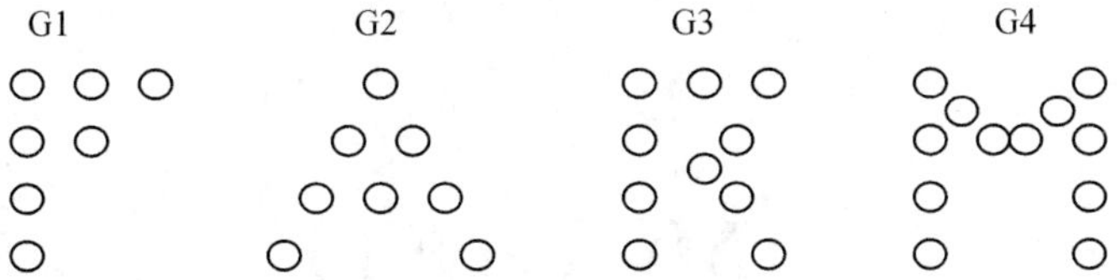

Step 5：Homework

1. Make sentences with “favourite”.

2. Listen to the tape and repeat.

3. Write the composition “My Favourite Animal”.

【活动评述】

在网上，找到与授课内容相关的动感画面，与教材有机的结合。学生不仅学习了句型“What’s your favourite animal?”而且扩大了视野，从情感上对动物有了更多的了解。他们更喜欢动物了，更愿意与动物交朋友了。如果挖掘资源、开发资源、好好地利用资源，那么我们的课堂会更精彩！

【资料链接】

1. http：//www.bbc.com

2. On the farm，Book 4，*Primary English for China*

（深圳市南山区北京师范大学附属小学　梁　冰）

My Pet (1)

【设计理念】

本设计通过介绍宠物商店，训练学生的发散性思维及观察能力；通过角色扮演，力求锻炼学生的交际能力，让他们在实践过程中充分感受到成功的喜悦，从而形成积极的学习态度，并促进语言实际运用能力的提高；通过小组的协作学习，培养学生自主运用语言的能力，并使其领悟到协作精神的重要性。

【活动目标】

1. 学生能将本课所学句型自如地运用到日常生活中，并熟悉所学的单词。

2. 通过角色扮演这一环节，培养学生的情境交际能力，并使其充分地感受到成功的喜悦。

3. 利用对话"Thank you!""Welcome to…"逐步培养学生的文明礼貌习惯。

4. 培养学生对英语的兴趣，让他们养成听、说英语的习惯。

【活动准备】

单词卡片，动物头饰，玩具动物，一个宠物商店的招牌，一些表示价钱的卡片，课件等。

【活动过程】

Step 1：Greetings

T：Good morning，boys and girls.

Ss：Good morning，Miss Liu.

T：Nice to meet you.

Ss：Nice to meet you，too.

T：I'm happy today. Are you happy today?

Ss：Yes，we are happy.

T：Very good! Let's sing the song If You Are Happy.

Step 2：Review

Ask some students to come to the front to be small teachers. 出示单词卡片，利用问答形式复习本课所学单词：cat，dog，bird，rabbit，turtle，fish，fly，swim 等。

"小老师"问：What's that?

全班回答：It's a cat.

"小老师"问：What can you see?

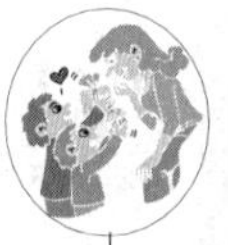

小组回答：We can see a turtle.

"小老师"问：What color is it?

个别学生回答：It's green.

"小老师"问：Do you like it?

个别学生回答：Yes，I do. / No，I don't.

"小老师"问：How many rabbits can you see?

个别学生回答：I can see…

Step 3：Presentation

Stage 1：教师演示课件，并以介绍的形式引导学生观看宠物店里的宠物。

Stage 2：以开火车问答的形式进行操练。

Stage 3：游戏：听动物的叫声，猜动物的名称。

Stage 4：教师出示玩具动物，学生模仿动物并各自说出一个句子。

Stage 5：叫一些学生带动物头饰模仿动物并进行自我介绍。

Stage 6：范例：教师利用宠物商店的招牌、玩具动物和一些表示价钱的卡片，布置一间卖宠物玩具的小商店。请学生配合：一人扮演商店售货员；三人扮演游客去购物。

Stage 7：分小组模仿范例编演小故事。老师给每个小组都准备一些表示价钱的小卡片，学生利用他们自带的玩具动物就可以自设场景进行角色扮演。

Step 4：Role-play

一年级学生表现欲极强，热情高涨，为了给同学们均等的机会，老师可以让各小组同时表演，自己巡视观看，对表演精彩的小组给予及时的奖励，对有进步的小组给予表扬，对有困难的小组给予帮助。

Step 5：Sum Up

教师总结本节课所学的内容，总评学生的学习活动，对有进步的学生给予奖励，并布置作业。

【活动评述】

本设计根据一年级学生好奇心强的心理特征，利用多媒体课堂创设英语语言教学情境，采用多种有效的教学方法，让学生在欢乐的气氛中学习。创设让学生观看动物、认识动物、扮演动物、购买动物的活动，使课堂学习充满了活力，而学生的学习兴趣得到极大地提高。课堂上始终以听说为主，整个学习气氛浓，教学效果好。

【资料链接】

1.《小学英语课程标准(实验稿)》，北京师范大学出版社，2001

2. My pet，Book 2，*Primary English for China*

（深圳市南山区南头城小学　刘丽玲）

My Pet (2)

【设计理念】

在小学英语学习的初始阶段，培养学生的说话能力和技巧，有利于拓展他们的思维。本设计围绕教学重点(认识并喜爱动物或宠物)，从说的多种表现形式(如 riddles，songs)来训练学生的创新思维，使他们多元化地运用语言，最终真正灵活地生成和转化语言。

【活动目标】

1. 使学生敢于开口说，有兴趣开口说。
2. 使学生的语言思维得到拓展，使他们的说话形式多元化。
3. 学生利用所学过的动词和形容词具体地描绘动物和宠物。

【活动准备】

1. 网上下载各种动物或宠物的图片，教师也可以自画图片。
2. 把下载的图片先编写成几个小谜语，用卡纸先写好或利用电脑幻灯片打好。例如：

I like this pet.
It's white.
It's small.
It has long ears.
It can jump.
It can run.
But It can't swim.
What is this?
谜底写在卡纸背面(It's a rabbit)。

3. 让学生自带一些动物或宠物的布娃娃或玩具。

【活动过程】

Step 1：Warming-up Exercises

1. Play a guessing game：利用 gesture 或宠物和动物的叫声来演示一种宠物，让学生猜测是什么，学生答对了就把图片贴在黑板上。重复多次，直到把所学的宠物都复习一遍，再让学生齐读这些单词。

2. Pair work：让学生两人一组做口头对话练习，一人扮演动物，另一个人猜。

这样既复习了所学单词又让学生互学互练，而以猜的形式激发了学生说的兴趣，真正让学生动手、动口又动脑。

3. 教师指着黑板上贴好的动物或宠物的卡片(或展示在电脑里)，与学生进行对话。

T：I like this pet. What colour is it?

Ss：It's yellow/ blue/ black…

T：Is it big? (small，tall，thin，fat，shot…)

Ss：Yes，it's big…

T：What can it do?

Ss：It can swim. (fly，jump，run，eat，drink…)

Step 2：Practice

1. 把电脑的幻灯片或写好谜语的纸片展示出来，如：

I like this pet.

It's small.

It's brown.

It can swim.

But it can't run.

It can't run.

It can't jump.

让学生齐读出来或个别学生朗读出来，再让学生当作 riddle 猜：What's this? 学生显得很活跃，都争先恐后指出谜底：It's a turtle.

2. 老师趁机引入自编谜语的口语活动训练，并提出让学生参照此形式进行自编谜语的比赛。让四个学生组成一组，每小组选择一种宠物或动物(当然是老师没有编过的宠物)，合作编口头谜语。

3. 自编活动完后，老师便让每个小组口头复述他们的谜面。做法是：先让小组成员每人说一句，再让小组长整篇的复述，最后让其他组的同学猜。这样不仅小组成员之间得到交流，而且小组与小组之间也进行了口头的交流。

4. 为了活跃课堂气氛，老师用课件和录音机播发有关宠物的英语歌。如：

I like the small cat.

I like it very much.

It can eat.

It can drink.

And it can run.

教歌时除了展示歌词外，教师最好同时扮演小宠物，做一些肢体动作。

5. 教师让学生把带来的玩具宠物拿在手上，并根据歌谣的曲调，把宠物唱出来。如：

I like the small fish.

I like it very much.

It can eat.

It can drink.

And it can swim.

6. 最后可进行交换宠物玩具的活动。教师让学生自由找同学交换玩具，规则是：只要能把另一同学手里的宠物玩具用歌曲的形式唱出来，就算成功交换。

【活动评述】

这是一个拓展式口头训练的活动设计。其中设计之精、教学之妙主要表现在：

1. 将思维训练和口语训练有机地结合起来。利用多种语言形式，激发了学生的创造性思维，也训练了学生的口头表达能力。

2. 敏锐捕捉和精心发掘思维训练点。学生自编谜语、自编歌曲，从易到难、从简单到复杂，都能循序渐进地过渡。

3. 所设计的活动新颖有趣。整节课里，生生之间、师生之间都进行了语言互动，学之有味、说之有趣。学生们最后在一片欢歌笑语中得到了心爱的玩具宠物。

【资料链接】

1. 《英语课程标准(实验稿)》，北京师范大学出版社，2001

2. My pet, Book 2, *Primary English for China*

(深圳市南山区大冲小学　刘梅超)

On the Farm (4)

【设计理念】

基础教育阶段英语课程的任务之一是锻炼学生的思维，培养学生的想像能力和创新精神。根据教学的重点内容进行创造性的说话训练，可以使学生巧妙地重组新旧知识，丰富语言的输出，从而真正达到灵活运用语言的目的。

【活动目标】

会说单词 pig，sheep，horse，cow，duck，chicken，并能灵活运用这些单词到不同的语境中。

【活动准备】

录音机，教师、学生自带玩具动物若干。

【活动过程】

Step 1：Lead In

T：(出示装有一玩具猪的不透明的塑料袋)Look at my plastic bag. There's a toy animal in it. Do you know what it is?

S1：Is it a dog?

S2：Is it a cat?

S3：Is it a rabbit?

T：The animal is on the farm.(露出玩具猪的一小部分给学生看)

S4：Oh, I know, it's a pig.

T：Yes, you are right. It's a lovely pig.(展示玩具猪给学生看)Today we will study the animals on the farm…

"猜测"这一游戏活动符合小学生好奇的心理特征。模糊的猜测对象激活了学生的思维，打开了学生的记忆闸门，激发了学生说的欲望。由此，教师巧妙地复习了以前所学的动物名称，导出了本课要学的语言知识。

Step 2：Competition

T：(出示一玩具鸭)Look, there's a duck. It's lovely. What colour is it? It's yellow…

Now let's have a competition. Let's try to say something about the animals. The more you say, the better you are. Let's see which group is the winner. OK. Let's begin with "duck".

黑板上记录各组造句的数量。

S1：The duck is lovely.

S2：I can see a yellow duck.

S3：I like eating ducks.

S4：May I have one duck，please?

…

T：Well done. Now，let's make some sentences wich "chicken".

S1：The chicken is fat.

S2：I eat chicken's legs in KFC.

S3：How many chickens are there?

…

教师可组织集体评价，并给优胜组奖励小红旗。

让学生对直观的实物造句，可以拓展学生的思维，激发学生的创造意识和语言联想，从而促进旧知识向新知识的迁移。学生获得了充足的自由想像的空间，要造出新句子也就不再难了。

Step 3：Group Work

T：Now please take out your toy animals. This time let's make dialogues about the animals. We'll do it in groups. Please get ready. Then I will ask some groups to come to the front and act out your dialogues.

Ss：(纷纷拿出自己的玩具，四人一小组积极地进行讨论和练习……)

T：Now Group 1，come to the front and act，please.

Group 1 —— Visiting the farm (学生把玩具摆放在讲台前面不同的地方)。

S1：Welcome to my farm.

S2：How many pigs are there on your farm?

S1：There are two pigs.

S3：Are there any sheep?

S1：Yes，there are four.

S4：What do your ducks eat?

S1：They eat fish.

Group 2 ——Shopping(学生把玩具全摆放在讲台上)。

S1：Can I help you?

S2：Yes. May I have one pig，please?

S1：Yes，here you are. Ten yuan，please.

S3：May I have two chickens，please?

S1：Yes，here you are. Twelve yuan，please.

S4：May I have one horse，please?

S1：Yes，here you are. Five yuan，please.

…

教师可组织全班评价，并给表演好的小组奖励小红旗。

小组合作创编对话，使学生的想像力、创造力得到了最大限度的释放和发挥。爱表演、好胜心强的心理特征促使各小组的成员群策群力、集思广益，从而培养了他们的合作精神。学生创造性地活化了所学的单词，编出了奇思妙想的对话，而且表演得惟妙惟肖，真正成了积极参与、自主创新的学习主体。

Step 4：Question

T：I'm very glad you did so well today. Now class will be over，what do you want to say to these animals?

S1：Little pig，why are you fat?

S2：What do you do on the farm，little sheep?

S3：Let's play，little chicken.

S4：How do you come to our school，horse?

S5：I love you，little sheep.

S6：How old are you，little duck?

S7：May I have your milk，cow?

S8：Can I help you，little sheep?

…

一个简单的问题点燃了无数学生创新思维的火花，激发了他们说的欲望，从而拓展了教材的内容。

【活动评述】

这是一个创造性说的活动设计。其设计之妙在于每一项活动都能激活学生的思维、激发学生的语言联想，使他们能积极、主动地重组新旧知识，从而活化所学的语言。学生觉得有话可说、有话想说，创新的火花自然而然地迸发了。

【资料链接】

1.《英语课程标准(实验稿)》，北京师范大学出版社，2001 年

2.《中小学英语教学与研究》，华东师范大学，2003 年第 8 期，第 10 期

3. On the farm，Book 4，*Primary English for China*

（深圳市南山区月亮湾小学　刘小惠）

At the Market (1)

【设计理念】

任务型教学(Task-Based Learning，简称 TBL)从新课程的精神出发，突出以人为本的思想，突出实践性和体验性原则，着眼于学生综合运用语言能力的培养，变知识性的课堂教学为发展性的课堂教学，充分体现课程改革的特征。在教学中，我们采用 TBL，把英语学习和有趣的游戏活动结合起来。在轻松有趣的学习活动中，学生的学习取得了事半功倍的效果。

【活动目标】

1. 通过真实、自然的语境，帮助学生巩固所学的单词：leafy vegetables，potatoes，cabbages，beans，onions，tomatoes.

2. 学习、练习和掌握新句型：(1) How much are the…?

(2) These / Those…are three yuan a kilo.

(3) May I have two kilos，please?

3. 鼓励学生多使用已学的礼貌用语。例如：Please! Sorry! Thank you. Thanks a lot. Can I help you? What can I do for you? You are welcome. Here you are. Bye—bye. See you. etc.

【活动准备】

将全班分为几个小组。每组一名学生为售货员，一名学生为监督员，剩余的学生为顾客。活动开展前的准备工作如下：

1. 用电脑展示蔬菜图片，帮助学生复习已学的英语蔬菜单词。

2. 准备一段外国朋友在超市购买蔬菜的真实录像。

3. 在表格一中的商品仅供参考。

表格一：出售商品一览表

Item / Serial Number	Vegetables	School Things	Drinks	Fruits	Toys
1	Leafy Vegetable	Pencil Case	Mineral Water	Banana	Toy Robot
2	Potatoes	Pencil	Coca Cola	Orange	Toy Doll
3	Cabbages	Rubber	Lemonade	Lychee	YoYo Ball
4	Beans	Ruler	Pepsi	Pear	Toy Bricks
5	Onions	Bag	Seven Up	Apple	Toy Train
6	Tomatoes	Pen	Smart	Peach	Toy Car

注：因为在新句型中会用到“These… / Those…”，所以每组必须准备双分不同价格的某种商品。

4. 各小组事先准备好两倍于小组人数的实物，并在实物上标好价格。

5. 各小组还需准备一个简易“柜台”。

6. 角色的要求。

(1) 售货员：用热情的服务态度去迎接每一位顾客。

(2) 监督员：认真地听售货员与顾客的对话，耐心地帮助有错误或有困难的顾客，记录商品的出售详细情况，并在活动结束后对本组表现进行公正的评价。

(3) 顾客：做一名文明、礼貌的消费者。

7. 准备一定的现金，如售货员的备用金 30 元，每位顾客的消费金额 10 元等。(考虑到活动的真实性，所以采用现金购买商品，让学生真实地感受购物)

8. 消费登记表格。

表格二(由监督员登记)

Item / Serial Number	Salesman (name)	Customer (name)	Merchandise (name)	Amount	Unit Price	Sum total
1						
2						
3						
4						
5						
6						
7						

表格三(由每一位顾客填写)

Customer	Salesman	Merchandise	Amount	Unit Price	Sum Total	Surplus

【活动过程】

1. 电脑展示图片，帮助学生复习已学单词。

Cabbages

Beans

Leafy Vegetables

Tomatoes

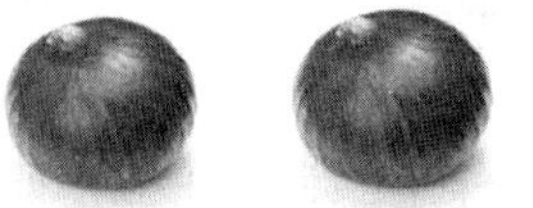

Onions

Potatoes

2. 播放外国朋友在超市购物的真实录像，引出今日所要学的新句型：

(1) How much are the…?

(2) These / Those…are three yuan a kilo.

(3) May I have two kilos, please?

3. 每组学生分别介绍自己组所出售的商品，教师和其他组学生共同参与商品价格的询问。

What are these? / What are those?

They are potatoes. They are onions.

How much are the potatoes / onions?

These potatoes / Those onions are three / four yuan a kilo.

4. 自由买卖商品。售货员站在柜台前(负责出售商品)；监督员站在柜台旁(负责监听售货员与顾客之间的对话是否正确，并记录商品的出售情况)；顾客自由购物。例如：

A friend of customer 1: Hello. Where are you going?

Customer 1: I'm going to the market.

A friend of customer 1: See you.

Customer 1: Bye.

Assistant: What can I do for you, Sir / Miss?

Customer 1: I'd like some tomatoes. How much are the tomatoes?

Assistant: These tomatoes are three yuan a kilo.

Those tomatoes are four yuan a kilo.

Customer 1: I want the tomatoes of three yuan a kilo. May I have two kilos, please?

Assistant: Ok, here you are.

Customer 1: How much is it?

Assistant: It's six yuan, please.

Customer 1: Here you are. Thanks a lot.

Assistant: You are welcome. Please wait a moment. Here's your change.

Customer 1: Thanks. Bye.

Assistant: Bye. Welcome next time.

每位学生均可套用以上句型，也可适当增减，酌情而定。最先售完货物的小组为优胜组。

表格在活动中的用途：(1) 监督员统计该组出售商品的情况；(2) 顾客在买完商品

后有一定的空闲时间，填表格不但可以保持他们的注意力不分散，还加强了他们的笔头表达能力；也便于现金的收回。

奖励方式：根据监督员的汇报，总结活动成绩，评出一、二、三名，并进行相应的奖励。

【活动评述】

这个活动设计有三个明显的特点：一是教师创设真实的情景，贴近现实生活，让学生在真实的环境中边玩边学语言。二是教师注重参与，并在活动中为每位学生都设计了角色。三是教师关注个体。教师在活动设计中关注每一位学生，尊重学生的个体差异，调动起每一位学生学习英语的积极性，让每一位学生在各自的基础上都有进步、有所得。

【资料链接】

1. Willis, J (1998), Task-Based Learning, English Teaching Professional

2. Harmer, J (1999), Question the Value of Language Study, English Teaching Professional

（深圳市南山区大新小学　刘　旭）

My Body

【设计理念】

培养学生学习英语的兴趣、激发他们学习英语的积极性是基础教育英语教学的主要任务之一。本教学活动设计力求打破传统课堂教学的“平静”和“呆板”，把语言教学精心安排在几个教学活动中，让学生在快乐的游戏活动里边玩边学习英语。

【活动目标】

1. 熟悉身体各部分的名称并能用英语说出来。

2. 能听懂英语课堂用语，对老师的指令（如 Open/Close/Touch 等）能做出正确的反应。

3. 学会使用陈述句“This is my…” “I can…”。

4. 初步具有课堂合作精神，乐于并善于参加各种形式的活动。

【活动准备】

铺地毯的活动场所；数张画有人体五官四肢的图片；一个动画故事片 My Five Senses；手工操作用小剪刀、白纸和膠水；小鼓或铃当。

【活动过程】

Step 1：Lead In

师生共唱歌曲“If You Are Happy”。

Step 2：Preparation

采用直观教学法让学生初步掌握以下内容。

单词：head，shoulder，knee，toe，eye，ear，hand，mouth，nose，foot，hair，body，arm，leg 等。

句子：Here's…I have…I can see with my eyes 等。

Step 3：Activities

1. Kid connections

Each child finds a partner. The teacher gives orders：“Toe to toe! Hand to hand! Knee to knee!” Each child says the sentences “This is my toe/hand/knee.” “Here's my toe/hand/knee.” and connects with his partner as quickly as possible. Then the teacher tries to give more difficult orders “hand to shoulder.” “leg to arm”.

小朋友们可喜欢这个游戏了。一些调皮的孩子在游戏结束后还意犹未尽地说“Mouth to mouth” “Mouth to face” “Mouth to ear” 等句子，逗得全班都乐开了花。

2. Body match-up

The teacher beats a drum, or rings a bell and says: "You walk and you walk and you walk and you stop!" After the teacher stops and calls out a body part "Hands!", the children have to match their hands each other. The teacher can change the action.

这个游戏增加了一些表示动作的词，难度增大了，它要求学生有一定的听的能力和肢体语言的快速反应能力。

3. Chant

This is my nose/ mouth. (Clap, clap, clap)
This is my nose/ mouth. (Clap, clap, clap)
It is red. It is red.
This is my nose/ mouth. (Clap, clap, clap)

4. My five senses

通过故事片的学习，学生们掌握了 I can see with my eyes. I can hear with my ears. I can touch with my hands. I can smell with my nose. I can tastes with my tongue 等内容。最后让学生了解 My five senses 是 taste, touch, smell, hear 和 see。通过学习，学生得出 Whatever I do, I use my five senses 的结论。

5. Changing body game

Give every pupil a picture. Let pupils cut off the body part of animals, people… and say: "Cut the head. Cut the hand." Then they can place them over their picture to see what they would look like in someone else's body! Finally they glue it to a piece of paper and say: "Stick the head. Stick the hand."

For example, let a pupil cut the head off of the clown and place the rest over the body of someone else's picture.

教室里弥漫着悠扬的乐曲声，小朋友们一个个趴在地毯上忙开了，他们口里说着英语，双手忙个不停。

【活动评述】

在本次活动设计中，老师讲的少了，学生的活动多了；师生单向的交流少了，学生之间、师生之间的互动和合作多了。老师是一个组织者和参与者，他们真正成为学习的主人，他们积极地参与每一教学环节，情绪高昂，切身感受了学习英语的快乐，品尝了成功的喜悦。教师真正做到了突出学生主体，关注学生发展。

【资料链接】

1.《英语课程标准(实验稿)》，北京师范大学出版社，2001 年

2. My body, Book 1, *Primary English for China*

（深圳市南山实验学校　卢桂娟）

Pet Corner

【设计理念】

活动教学是让学生在感知的基础上，通过体验、实践、参与、合作与交流的方式，实现学习任务的目标。我们只有从组织教学活动入手，大量地进行语言实践，使英语课堂交际化，才能有效地培养学生运用英语进行交际的能力；才能在培养学生语言能力的同时，开发学生的智力，发挥他们的潜能和创造精神。

【活动目标】

1. 通过活动，掌握所学动物的名称及它们吃、喝的食物名。

2. 能抓住动物的特征和习性，用英语进行简单的口头描述，并在参与、合作和竞争中体验英语学习的成功与喜悦。

3. 了解更多的动物，具有初步的环保意识。

【活动准备】

1. 已经认识相关动物和颜色词。

2. 动物及食物图片。

3. 白纸、彩色笔等(学生自己准备)。

【活动过程】

Step 1：Lead In

运用动物图片、彩色笔等复习所学动物的英语名称、颜色词(以“开火车”的形式让学生用英语大声地说出动物名和颜色词)及“This is…” “It eats…” 等句型。

Step 2：Competition

全班分成四组(按平时的座位安排来分)，并在黑板的最上方写出：

Group 1 　Group 2 　Group 3 　Group 4

教师首先讲清楚竞赛方法和规则：回答正确后，在黑板上相应组的位置画出一颗小红星给予鼓励，回答错误的不画标志。

1. 第一轮比赛开始。教师让某一个学生分别模仿动物狗、猫、鸟、鸭、猪、青蛙等的叫声，要求其他学生根据叫声来判断，并用英语说出该动物的名称。教师和学生共同评价，同时给抢答成功者所在的小组一颗小红星予以鼓励。

2. 第二轮比赛继续。让某一个学生分别模仿相关动物的动作，其他学生根据自己看到的动作来判断，并用英语说出该动物的名称(方式也可以是抢答)。同样，教师要注意评价，给优胜者一颗小红星作为鼓励。

3. 第三轮比赛是四人小组活动。先让每小组用最快的速度画一张自己所喜爱的动物简图，并想好怎样用英语进行描述（要求在1～2分钟内完成）。如：

This is my rabbit. It's white. It eats carrots and drinks water. I like my rabbit. Do you like it?

然后选派代表用英语向全班口头描述。最后教师简洁明了地进行评价，并给予鼓励。

4. 第四轮比赛在第三轮比赛的基础上进行猜谜。学生举手用英语口头描述某一动物的主要特征，其他学生进行抢答。教师分别奖给描述者、猜中谜底者两颗星和一颗星。

例：I have a pet. It hasn't feet and hands, but it can swim very well.

What is it? (fish)

Step 3：End

看哪一组获得的小红星最多就是这次活动的获胜者。鼓励学生在课后继续猜动物谜，有条件的学生可以上网查阅我国珍稀动物的有关资料。

【活动评述】

活动设计抓住小学生好胜心强的心理特点，开展多种形式的竞赛。竞赛活跃了气氛，既有利于培养学生思维的敏捷性，又有利于增强学生的责任感和集体荣誉感。在小组你追我赶、竞相达标的过程中，学生们充分发挥动态的集体力量。当然，教师要掌握好评分技巧和灵活的评价手段，使竞赛锦上添花。

【资料链接】

1.《英语课程标准（实验稿）》，北京师范大学出版社，2001年

2. 我国珍稀动物网址：http://free.7host02.com/bxcai

3. Pet corner, Book 6, *Primary English for China*

（深圳市南山区向南小学　马　达）

Helping at Home (2)

【设计理念】

本教学活动设计——家务活，与我们的日常生活紧密相关。活动模拟真实的情境，并设计形象具体的活动来让学生开口说英语。本设计力求通过各种各样的学生很喜欢的活动，达到语言训练的反复，让学生在轻松活泼愉快的环境中完成学习的任务。

【活动目标】

1. 学习一些常见的家务活的英语表达法：sweep the floor，wash the dishes，clean a room，set the table，make the bed，water the plants 等。能够将这些词组与 can 或现在进行时结合在句子中根据实际情况进行运用，如：I can sweep the floor. I'm sweeping the floor 等。

2. 培养学生大胆表现自己，敢说英语的信心。

3. 让学生热爱家庭，并积极参与劳动、尊重劳动、热爱劳动。

【活动准备】

实物：扫帚，纸碟子，花壶，假盆花，小床单，单词卡片；课件：用 PowerPoint 做好的 chant。

【活动过程】

Step 1：Guessing Game

老师做洗脸动作，学生说动词 wash；做炒菜动作，学生说 cook……依次复习已学的动词。教师接着拿扫帚做扫地动作，引出 sweep the floor 的句型，依次用实物和动作导入新词组，并将它们分别写到黑板上。

Step 2：Listen and Read

学生听录音，并进行跟读(借助单词卡读)。教师让学生将卡片画面朝上，并分别用磁铁贴到黑板上相应的英文词组的上面，从而对单词的形和意有初步的记忆。

Step 3：Chant and Act

老师在屏幕上展示 chant 的第一节，并让学生跟自己一边有节奏地说唱，一边做动作。

Sweep the floor，sweep the floor，

Can you sweep the floor?

Yes，I can.

Yes，I can.

I can sweep the floor.

接着用 wash the dishes 替换：

Wash the dishes, wash the dishes,

Can you wash the dishes?

Yes, I can.

Yes, I can.

I can wash the dishes.

男女轮流对答：

Boys：Clean a room, clean a room. Can you clean your room?

Girls：Yes, I can. Yes, I can. I can clean my room.

依次以轮流问答的形式往下进行，从而让学生加深对新单词的形、音、意的印象。

Step 4：Quick Reaction

通过上一个活动，学生已进入状态，这时就利用 flash cards 进行快速反应。老师将卡片有图画的一面在学生面前迅速展示一下，要求学生马上说出相应的词组。

Quick reaction 这一环节会让学生变得更加兴奋。老师也可以借此检查大部分学生掌握单词读音的情况。但是学生一起回答，会有一些滥竽充数的学生躲在里面不被发现。所以，可以进行两大组之间的比赛，如男女竞赛，并采取爬格子的奖励办法。每次每组分别派一名代表参赛，谁先准确无误地说出单词，谁就上一格，先拿到格子顶端的红旗的组获胜。但这样参与面就没有那么广，且比较费时。

Step 5：Mime Game

Pair work：学生两两配合，一个说“Jenny, sweep the floor, please.”或“Jenny, wash the dishes, please.”一个做相应的动作，轮流进行表演。

Step 6：Question Chain

老师提问一学生，学生回答后再问另一个学生，一直接下去：

T：I can sweep the floor. What can you do?

S1：I can water the plants. What can you do?

S2：I can set the table. What can you do?

…

学生很喜欢接龙问答的方式，个个都把手举得高高的，希望同学能点到自己。这个环节能给学生一个在全班同学面前展示自己的机会。很多学生会一连串地列出很多家务活：I can make my bed, sweep the floor and water the plants. But I can't wash the dishes. 这样，语言的灵活性和多样性就出来了。

Step 7：Play House

在现在进行时的句子中运用新词组。教师将带进课室的实物在讲台周围分布好：将扫帚放在讲台旁边，说：“This is the living room.”将床单放在讲台上，说：“This is the bedroom.”依次布置好阳台、饭厅、厨房。告诉学生：“This is a flat. There is a family in the flat. There are Grandpa, Grandma, Dad, Mum, and Tim.”老师先做个示范，拿起盘子，做洗碗动作，说：“I'm Mum. I'm in the kitchen. I'm washing the dishes.”叫六名学生上台，分别扮演爷爷、奶奶、爸爸、妈妈和 Tim 在不同的房间里做家务活。S1拿起水壶做浇花动作，说："I'm Grandpa. I'm at the balcony. I'm watering the plants." S2拿起扫帚说："I'm Grandma. I'm in the living room. I'm sweeping the floor."……

【活动评述】

兴趣是最好的老师。这堂课教师设计了很多动手做和动口说的活动，让学生不知不觉地在游戏中反复操练新单词而不觉得枯燥乏味，同时给每一位学生单独说和做的机会，整个课堂轻松而愉快。

【资料链接】

1.《英语课程标准(实验稿)》，北京师范大学出版社，2001年

2. Helping at home, Book 6, *Primary English for China*

（深圳市南山区南山小学　陈　虹）

At Home (3)

【设计理念】

单词是个枯燥的个体,如果孤立地去教学生怎样读、怎样写或怎样运用,那么学生所能掌握到的只是个单词而已。怎样使课文中的每个单词具有长久的、鲜活的生命力?让学生融进熟悉的生活活动中去,并在活动过程中体验不同的角色,体会不同的感受,就能唤起学生积极主动学习的愿望和兴趣,从而达到掌握知识要点的目的。

【活动目标】

1. 学习描述家庭设施的单词和短语,如:kitchen, living room 等。
2. 学习描述家庭生活的句子,如:I can cook. I'm cooking in the kitchen 等。
3. 培养学生我爱我家的情感。

【活动准备】

教师课前准备各种角色的头饰和一些生活用品。

【活动过程】

Step 1: Lead In

老师以录像的形式向学生们介绍自己的家庭。

师:同学们,这是我的家。刚才镜头里都拍了哪些地方?每个小组至少说出两个内容。

生:客厅、卧室、洗手间、书房、厨房……

各组分别把刚才看到的内容一一讲出来,老师顺势在黑板上逐次贴出相应的图片。

师:床→卧室 bed→bedroom

洗澡→浴室 bath→bathroom

……

生:卧室与床有关,浴室与洗澡有关,这样就好记了。

师:再想想刚才镜头中出现的动作有哪些?

生:卧室里睡觉,洗手间里洗手,厨房里做饭,客厅里看电视(学生争先恐后地举手发言)。

师:好,大家观察得很仔细,现在看黑板上老师总结的内容:

床→卧室→睡觉→在卧室→爷爷在卧室睡觉

bed→bedroom→sleep→in the bedroom→Grandpa is sleeping in the bedroom

冲凉→冲凉房→洗手→在冲凉房→奶奶在冲凉房洗衣服

bath→bathroom→wash→in the bathroom→Grandma is washing in the bathroom

厨房→做饭→叔叔在厨房做饭

kitchen→cook→Uncle is cooking in the kitchen

……

这一活动用生动形象而具体的内容，使学生自然而然地接触到新单词的应用环境。同时教师把人物适当地引入进来，一句完整的话就顺利完成。

Step 2：Role-play

经过新单词的拼读和句子的变化，学生已经能够较流利地念出词和句。为使他们加深印象，教师可以采用让学生亲身体验的办法。

师：我的爸爸妈妈为了支持我的工作，主动帮忙照看我的女儿和料理家务。现在请同学上来带上爷爷、奶奶的头饰进行角色扮演。

生：I'm old. But I can help you. I can cook. I'm cooking in the kitchen.

生：I'm a happy Grandma. I can sing. I can dance. I'm washing and singing in the bathroom. Everybody calls me Happy Grandma.

师：刚才的同学扮演得真棒，用词好，句子也正确。看看有谁挑战他们。

生：I'm an old teacher. I'm an English teacher. I like to play badminton. I'm reading in the living room.

生：I love my family. I like to watch TV. I'm watching TV in the bedroom. I'm tired now. I'm going to sleep.

师：太好了，同学们都表演得很好，现在我们一起总结刚才用过的词汇。（在黑板上写出相应的新单词）

Step 3：Review

把课文中表示地点的单词卡片以及与旧知识相关的卡片贴在黑板的上一层，把课文中表示动作的单词卡片以及与旧知识相关的卡片贴在黑板的下一层，让学生熟练地将词、句与相对应的图片连接起来。

老师准备好卧室、餐厅、客厅、教室、操场、厨房、电脑教室、洗手间及学习、睡觉、玩游戏、做饭、洗衣服、看电视、喝饮料、打篮球等卡片。

师：谁能把黑板上的地点图片与动作图片连接起来，并将他们说成一个完整的句子。（老师分别叫七八个学生来完成）

S1：My grandpa is sleeping in the bedroom.

S2：Tom is drinking in the dining room.

S3：That little girl is watching TV in the living room.

S4：The students are studying in the classroom.

S5：We are playing basketball in the playground.

S6：My mother is cooking in the kitchen.

S7：The boy is playing games in the computer room.

S8：My grandma is washing in the bathroom.

Step 4：Group Work

小组学习是很有效的学习手段，学生们在宽松的气氛中更能发挥出自己的能力。

师：以小组为单位，大家可根据自己的喜好扮演角色，比一比哪家更温馨。

学生各自准备，按自己理解的课文内容选择角色，然后在小组中扮演。

【活动评述】

这课的教学活动设计突破了以往传统的单词授课方法，教师灵活运用电视、图片、头饰等多种手段，使学生自然而然地接受新知识。教学过程轻松愉快，学生积极主动。教师在教学中还融进了情感教育，实现了教书和育人的有机结合。

【资料链接】

1.《英语课程标准(实验稿)》，北京师范大学出版社，2001 年

2. At home, Book 6, *Primary English for China*

（深圳市南山区南头城小学　陈桂萍）

At the Market (2)

【设计理念】

活动以实践为主，用直观的手段创设语言交际的情景，使学生将课堂知识与实际生活有效地结合。活动采用听、说、比的形式让学生完成从机械模仿到灵活交际的过程。设计持续强化语言技能，并通过真实的任务来完成教学的目标，让学生们快乐地分享课堂活动。

【活动目标】

1. 学生掌握蔬菜的英语单词和常用买卖用语。

2. 学生能够在购物的环境下自然、灵活、大胆地使用交际语言。

【活动准备】

1. 教师将学生分成若干组，让他们分别准备蔬菜（白菜、土豆、豆角、西红柿、洋葱等），但每人只准备一样（从妈妈买回的菜中取或自己用零钱去菜场买）。

2. 学生将所喜爱的游戏——“大富翁”中所用交易之钱币带入课堂，以作购物资金，并准备贴有不同价格的标签。

3. 教师准备一张围裙，几个购物塑料袋。

4. 教师准备一系列菜市场的 PowerPoint 图片和顾客在菜市场买菜的课件。

5. 教师准备一棵长满大红苹果的树（由彩色硬纸剪贴而成，每个苹果后写有孩子们所能想到的一些蔬菜英文单词）。

6. 教师发给学生每人一张 vote form（投票表），让他们投票选出心目中的最佳售货员、最佳顾客、最佳微笑、最佳语言表现奖。

【活动过程】

1. 师生互问好，借此引出主题。

T：Hello, boys and girls! How are you today? What day is today? What's the date today?

Ss：Hello, Miss Xu! We are fine. Today is Friday. It's Apr. 30th.

T：Yes. Next Sunday is the Mother's Day. I want to do something for my mother, so I will go to the market to buy some vegetables. Do you want to do this for your mother?

Ss：Sure.

T：OK, let's go.

2. Play the computer to show some flash photos of the market.

（用幻灯片将学生引入市场环境）

T：Look, here we are. What vegetables does your mother like? What vegetables do you know?

T：Here is an apple tree. There is a vegetable's name on each back of the apple. You can get the apple for your mother.（用苹果来导入交际所需的词汇）

3. 老师出示蔬菜的实物，竞价贴标签。（提出主要句型）

T：I bought some, can you guess how much they are?

鼓励学生大胆猜测，并询问价格是否合理，如果大家都可以接受，就让学生为其贴上价格标签。

Ss：How much are these/those? They are… yuan.（学生使用主要句型）

4. 给学生五分钟，让他们在小组内讨论，为自己带来的蔬菜贴上价格标签。（指导学生强化句型）

S1：How much are the tomatoes?

S2：These tomatoes are 10 yuan…

5. 给学生播放一段菜市场里售货员和顾客做买卖的课件。（再现实际环境，利于学生记忆交际句型）

Storekeeper：Excuse me. Can I help you?

The Customer：Yes, please. How much are those tomatoes?

Storekeeper：They're four yuan a kilo.

The Customer：How much are these tomatoes?

Storekeeper：They're three yuan a kilo.

The Customer：I want these tomatoes. May I have two kilos, please?

Storekeeper：Yes, here you are. It's six yuan.

The Customer：Thank you.

6. 教师将学生们预先存放的蔬菜摆出，让他们将想要买的蔬菜写在 shopping list 上。教师穿上售货员的围裙示范售货员，其他的同学做顾客。（向学生示范整个买卖过程，利于学生深化印象）

7. 让学生在小组内操练做买卖。（学生再次演练句型）

8. 每个小组派代表表现买卖情景。（学生展现语言交际过程）

9. 师生一起评价：看谁能顺利买到又多又好又便宜的蔬菜，并通过学生们交上来的投票表，评出该活动中的最佳售货员、最佳顾客和最佳微笑。

【活动评述】

用自己带来的蔬菜当教具，学生们都很兴奋，他们投入在假设的情景中，在任务的驱动下，自信而轻松地开口说英语。整个课堂气氛活跃，教学效果显著。

【资料链接】

1. 王电建、赖红玲，《小学英语教学法》，北京大学出版社，2002

2.《任务型语言教学——英语教学理论与实践丛书》，人民教育出版社，2003

3. 李庆，《成功教学的策略——有效的教学实习指南》，中国轻工业出版社，2002

4. Linda Campbell，《多元智能教与学的策略》，中国轻工业出版社，2001

5. At the market, Book 6, *Primary English for China*

（深圳市南山区南头城小学　徐雪梅）

My Pet (3)

【设计理念】

创设一个轻松愉快的课堂环境，让小孩子们边玩边学，着重培养他们学习英语的兴趣。引导学生去思考，着重培养学生运用语言的能力，让他们在“用”的过程中发展思维能力。

【活动目标】

1. 学生能够根据实物或卡片说出新单词。

2. 学生掌握新句型，能够用所学的句型描述实物。

【活动准备】

动物玩具：bird，rabbit，fish，dog，cat，turtle 等。

【活动过程】

1. 玩游戏说英语

游戏规则：把准备好的玩具依次抛给不同的学生，接到玩具的学生必须用英语说出玩具的名称，然后再造一个句子。

例如：

(Teacher throws a toy bird to a student)

T：What's this?

S1：It's a bird.

Bird，bird，bird——I like a bird.

(Teacher throws a toy rabbit to another student)

S2：Rabbit，rabbit，rabbit——That's a rabbit.

…

(通过实物帮助学生形象记忆)

设计使大部分学生有机会参与活动。教师可以对个别发音不准的学生给予及时的纠正。

2. 边说边做

教师让全班同学站起来，跟着自己边说边做。

T：Now boys and girls！ Stand up，please！ Follow me！

Fly，fly like a bird.

Swim，swim like a fish.

Jump, jump like a rabbit.

Miao, miao like a cat.

Walk, walk like a turtle.

这个边说边做的活动把本课所学的单词以朗朗上口的句式说出来，并配以形象的动作，大大地激发了学生们说英语的兴趣。

3. 小组比赛

把全班分成五个小组进行比赛。教师出示动物玩具，让学生用学过的句型来描述动物的特征、能力或表达自己的喜好。教师让学生在组内讨论，讨论后每组选出两名同学进行作答。说出的句型越多越正确的小组，所得的红花就越多。

T：Now, let's begin! (Show them a toy turtle)

Group 1

S1：This is my turtle. It's green.

S2：It's a turtle.

Group 2

S1：The turtle can swim. It can't run. It can't jump. It can't fly.

S2：It can't sing. It can't dance. It can't read. It can't write.

Group 3

S1：My turtle is on the desk.

S2：I like turtle. It's small.

Group 4

S1：My turtle is short. My turtle is thin.

S2：My turtle is in the toy box. My turtle is under the chair. Look at the turtle.

…

教师以比赛的形式，把表演的平台完全交给学生，让他们在教学活动中充当"说"的主角。

【活动评述】

随着新课程改革的日益深入，教师的教学方式、学生的学习方式，都在发生深刻的变化。英语的"说"不再是单纯的老师带读、学生跟读，更不是让学生机械式地重复，而是把生硬的、死板的、没有生命的文字性的东西，变得更加鲜活、更加丰富多彩。也就是说，把老师"要求说"，变成学生"想说""要说""敢说""乐说"。

【资料链接】

1.《英语课程标准(实验稿)》，北京师范大学出版社，2001 年

2. My pet, Book 2, *Primary English for China*

（深圳市南山区平山小学　陈丽雅）

My Day

【设计理念】

在新课程理念的指导下，教师要树立“面向全体学生，突出学生主体，尊重学生个体差异”的教学思想，让学生在轻松、民主、融洽、和谐的教学氛围中，进入教师给他们创设的各种真实半真实的语言环境，并在参与趣味性、知识性强的各类教学活动中，进行语言学习和语言交流，激发起学习英语的兴趣，建立成就感和自信心，以形成积极的学习态度，促进语言实际运用能力的提高。

【活动目标】

1. 学生熟练掌握时间的表达方法、表示日常生活和学习的常用短语及句型。

2. 学生对所学的内容有好奇心，乐于开口、敢于开口，并积极参与活动。

【活动准备】

1. 教师自备一个大钟表。

2. 学生配备剪刀、圆规、卡纸（硬纸板）、彩色笔、图钉。

3. 教师准备作息时间调查表。

4. 教师准备有关钟表的音乐或其他多媒体资料。

【活动过程】

Step 1：Lead In

1. 第一则有关钟表的谜语。

T：I am big, just like a box. I have a big face without a nose or eyes. I don't have any hands or legs. Everybody, old or young, likes to watch me. Do you know what I am?

刚听完开头两句，就有个别小家伙按捺不住了：

S1：Cupboard! It's a cupboard!

S2：No! Wardrobe! It's a wardrobe!

S3：No! It's a luggage!

…

2. 第二则有关钟表的谜语。

T：I have a big round face. I have no legs or feet, but I can walk. I have no mouth, but I can say “tick—tock' tick—tock”. What am I?

话音刚落，孩子们很快就将答案一致锁定在 clock 上。孩子们在恍然大悟中走出了迷局，但个个意犹未尽。

Step 2：Action

1. 学生比赛自制一个钟表。

在比赛的过程中，为了活跃气氛，播放两首有关钟表的少儿英文歌曲。

Are You Sleeping：Are you sleeping，are you sleeping，Brother John，Brother John? Morning bells are ringing，morning bells are ringing. Ding－dong－ding，ding－dong－ding.

Oh，How Lovely Is The Evening：Oh，how lovely is the evening，is the evening. When the bells are sweetly ringing，sweetly ringing. Ding，dong！Ding，dong！Ding，dong！

伴随着欢快、优美的旋律，和着熟悉、动听的曲调，小家伙们一边忙碌于制作，一边愉快地哼唱着，完全沉浸在快乐之中。

2. 向同学介绍自制的钟表。

S1：Look！My clock has a triangle face.

S2：My clock looks like a panda.

S3：My clock is a little house.

S4：Look at my clock. It has a round face，just like a watermelon. Do you like it?

小家伙们兴致勃勃地展示着他们的得意之作。

Step 3：Role-play

1. 利用自制钟表进行"老狼、老狼几点了"的小组游戏。

四人当中一位同学扮演大灰狼，其他三位扮演小羊。小羊们发问："老狼、老狼几点了?"老狼就要将自己的小钟表随意拨到一个钟点，并在出示给小羊们看的同时，用英语说出正确的时间。

S1：Wolf，wolf！What time is it?

S2：It's ten.

S3：Wolf，wolf ！What's the time?

S4：It's seven fifteen.

孩子们轮流扮演着小羊和大灰狼的角色，要是小羊一时性急问错了问题，大灰狼就会毫不留情地扑过去，把"她"抓过来做大灰狼，以替代自己"不光彩的角色"。可如果是大灰狼说错了时间，小羊就会勇敢地群起而攻之，罚"它"讲英语笑话或说一首韵律诗。

2. 教师在屏幕上呈现出两个圆圆的大西瓜，分别将其二分之一和四分之一涂成红色，来表达"half"和 "quarter"，介绍时间的另一种表达方式，并鼓励学生将其运用到他们的游戏活动中去。

Step 4：Practice

发放"学生作息时间调查表"：该表设计了起床、吃早餐、上学、吃午餐、放学、做作业、吃晚餐、上床睡觉等一系列有关孩子们一天作息的立体生活场景。教师在调查表旁边相对应的时钟上却故意省去了时针和分针，让孩子们两两结对互相问答：

S1：When do you…?

S2：I…at…

问方要根据答方所答的内容画出相应的时间。

【活动评述】

本设计力图改变传统的教学模式，开发“高效率学习英语兴趣化、组织过程情景化和活动形式多样化”的创新模式，使学生在画画、唱唱、说说、练练的活动中，真正成为课堂的小主人。

【资料链接】

1. 刘建华，《交际教学法实践》，学苑出版社，1999

2. 《英语辅导报》，小学教师版

3. My day, Book 6, *Primary English for China*

（深圳市南山区平山小学　刘　继）

Preparing Food

【设计理念】

让低年级学生开口说英语并不是一件很难的事情，倒是伴随开口而生的许多意想不到的问题会时常困扰教师。比如：孩子们常常发音不准；他们在练习英语单词或句型时，总会很快地退到母语状态，说些悄悄话。为克服这种退化现象，教师要尽可能地降低单词学习的枯燥性。考虑到新授教学阶段的特殊性，我们设计了哑巴式“打电话”“开火车”“单词迷宫”等活动，引导学生关注自己的发音方法和效果，弱化单词的视觉陌生感，进而维护学生学习英语的高度热情。

【活动目标】

1. 学生认识单词并基本掌握读音：tomato，lettuce，cheese，salad dressing，ham，cucumber 等。

2. 学生识别单词组合：tomato with eggs，ham with cucumber，ham with pineapple，chicken with lettuce 等。

3. 学生学会应用句型：How much is it? It's…yuan (dollars)。

【活动准备】

1. 单词卡片、模型和实物。

2. 磁带、录音机。

3. 奖品：小苹果、小橘子、小星星。

【活动过程】

Step 1：Rules

1. 全班分为三个队：苹果队、橘子队，教师。奖品分别对应为：小苹果、小橘子、小星星。

2. 通过哑巴式“打电话”“开火车”“猜单词”等三种形式开展两队之间的比赛。

3. “打电话”游戏开始的时候，每个接线员必须双手抱在一起，置于胸前；转身传递单词时，身体保持挺拔，不得趴到后边学生的耳朵上传递发音。接话的学生要用眼睛仔细看对方的嘴，模仿并猜测单词。违反规则一次，扣除一个奖品。

4. “开火车”游戏的过程中，每个队伍中推举或由教师任意选择一名学生，承担首个传递任务。如果该生听老师说一遍单词，就可以准确地重复出来，可得一个奖品；如果该生需要两次或更多次才能重复出老师说出的单词，则不能为本队赢得奖品。

5. “猜单词”阶段，其他成员可以不停地借助本队发言者的口型，求得无声的帮忙，但发出声音的队伍则得不到奖品。

6. 在“打电话”“开火车”“猜单词”的整个过程中，自从老师做出“zip our mouths”的动作后，包括老师在内，任何人都不可发出声音，只能默默地用嘴无声“说话”。在每个环节中，遵守规则者，得小红花一朵。

7. 在比赛的每个环节中，如果学生的两支队伍都没有猜出正确的单词，则奖品归老师。

例如：Orange　　　Apple　　　Teacher
　　　橘子图形　　　苹果图形　　　小星星图形

Step 2：Warm-up

由于 tomatoes，lettuce，cheese，salad dressing，ham，cucumber 对学生们来说，都是新单词，所以要设计前期热身练习，以保证后续活动的质量。

1. 出示图片、实物、模型，利用曾经学过的句型“What's this?”或“What are these?”等，引出 lettuce，tomatoes，cheese，salad dressing，ham，cucumber，eggs 等单词。这个阶段主要是老师给出标准的读音，学生进行跟读。老师告诉学生注意一边跟读发音，一边注意自己的口型变化。

2. 老师随机挑选单词，面向全体学生发音，但不出声，强调学生注意观察口型，并依据口型猜测单词。这个阶段，老师要给孩子们一定的时间，允许他们默默交流。

3. 打开录音机，播放单词的标准读音，鼓励学生放声跟读，进一步强化记忆。

Step 3：Telephone on Train

1. 老师做出“zip”指令，Orange、Apple、Teacher 队都进入“无声状态”。

2. 教师从每个队伍中挑选出一名学生，在其耳边悄悄说出某个单词，不让其他学生听到。

3. 教师用表情和口型发出“Get ready!”或“Are you ready?”的咨询，学生也以同样方式回馈“Yes”“No”或“Ok”。

4. 首个接受任务的学生同时转身，各自面向本队的第二个学生演示单词发音的口型，然后以此类推。

5. 每队最后接收单词的学生到老师处耳语，验证“打电话”“开火车”的效果，教师据此决定每个队的成绩。

6. 教师解除“无声状态”，任意抽查学生，鼓励他们大声说出刚才传递的单词，每个正确的读音都将为本队增添一个奖品。

Step 4：Shopping

1. Orange 和 Apple 队都分成两个小组，共为四组，每组八九个人：Orange I、Orange II、Apple I、Apple II。

2. 四个小组分别领取一种有关西红柿、生菜、奶酪、沙拉酱、黄瓜、菠萝、火腿、鸡蛋的图片、单词卡片、模型和实物。如：Orange I 选择图片、Orange II 选择实物、Apple I 选择单词卡片、Apple II 选择模型。

3. 领取到实物和模型的两个小组（Orange II、Apple II），要分别根据自己的材料，设计一个“农贸超市”，组内成员分别承担导购小姐（先生）、售货员、顾客和出纳等角色，并利用所学单词（tomatoes，lettuce，cheese，salad dressing，ham，cucumber），词组（tomato with eggs，ham with cucumber，ham with pineapple，chicken with lettuce）和句型（How much is it? It's…yuan/dollars）进行买卖活动。

4. 领取图片和单词卡片的两个小组(Orange I、Apple I),则要开展“单词匹配”的活动。

5. 四个小组分别交换材料,再次零距离对垒。

【活动评述】

教师与孩子们的“zip”约定,能在很大程度上制止他们退回到母语状态。好胜的心理总是促使学生非常认真而虔诚地看着老师、同学们的口型,谨慎地发音。再有一点,这种活动也可以调动孩子们的兴趣,即使平时课堂表现不积极的同学也会为了集体的荣誉感或受同伴的鼓舞而加入到学习中来。

【资料链接】

1.《英语课程标准(实验稿)》,北京师范大学出版社,2001 年

2. *Integreted Primary English Toc edition* (3A)

(深圳市南山区沙河小学　陈春红)

Learning Words on Internet

【设计理念】

新课程强调从学生的学习兴趣、生活经验和认识水平出发，倡导体验、实践、参与、合作与交流的学习方式，发展学生对语言的综合运用能力。本设计力求在单词教学的活动中通过信息技术与英语教学的整合，使学生能够在网络环境下进行自主学习，两两或小组合作学习，并在真实阅读情景中活跃思维、拓展视野。

【活动目标】

1. 让学生认读新单词及句型。
2. 培养学生爱护大自然的情感。

【活动准备】

1. 图、文、声三者结合的多媒体网络资源。
2. 动物头饰。
3. 单词卡片、图片。

an elephant	a panda	a lion	a giraffe	a monkey

a wolf	a dragon	a turtle	a tiger	a mouse

【活动过程】

第一部分

Step 1：Warm-up

1. 教师指着教室里的事物与学生对话：

T：What's this?

Ss：It's a fan(light/desk/chair/board…)

2. 学生指着自己的文具自我对话：

What's this/that? It's a ruler(rubber/pen/pencil…)

3. 师生进行互动游戏。

T：Look at your book…

Ss：(把手指贴在眼角并看着书)：Look at my book…

Step 2：New Words

1. 教师展示网络资源里图、文、声并茂的动物单词。

T：Boys and girls!

Ss：Yes.

T：Look at the pictures. Do you like the animals?

Ss：Yes.

T：OK，let's go to the computers and learn the words of the animals by ourselves.

学生通过 flash 自主学习本课的单词及拓展单词。本环节有助于培养学生自学的能力。

2. 教师帮助学生正音，以强化其认读单词的能力。(此时教师手中拿着动物图片)

T：Look at this picture. What's this?

Ss：It's an elephant.

T：How do you spell this word?

Ss：…

最后，教师把学生分为 A、B 两组，A 组问、B 组答或 B 组问、A 组答。

3. Pair work(学生两两说)。

教师给每组第一排的学生一张动物卡片，学生两两就所给的图片进行对话，第一排练完后就把图传给第二排，以此复习和巩固所学的单词，同时也培养学生合作学习的良好习惯。最后教师叫几对学生进行演示。

4. Guess the animals 的游戏。

教师把五张单词图片反放在黑板上，将学生分为四个小组，每组一次让一个学生站起来猜，猜中的话该小组可获得一颗红星，猜不中的话则轮到下一组猜。

T ：What's in the picture?

S1：It's a lion. / Is that a lion?

5. 学唱英文歌曲：

Where is the elephant? It's at the zoo…

6. 学生课后玩的网络游戏(flash)：

Where is the giraffe? Guess who I am. Pick a pet 等。

第二部分

Step 1：Warm-up

1. Sing an English song.

唱上一课时学唱的英文歌曲。

2. Everyday sentences.

让一个学生当小老师提出问题，其他学生进行回答；或学生们问，小老师答。

Step 2：Review

1. 全班看图片回答老师的问题。

T：What's this?

S1：It's a lion.

T：Can you see the panda?

S2：Yes，I can.

T：Can you see the elephant?

S3：No，I can't.

2. 造句复习所学的单词。

教师手拿一张单词卡片，先示范，如：

Look at this picture.

Look at the giraffe.

然后让学生进行模仿，造句复习所学的单词。

Step 3：Now Words

1. 通过复习水果及颜色单词引出本课新的颜色单词(附加图片道具)。

red	green	yellow	orange	brown
an apple	a pear	a banana	an orange	a horse
 purple		 red	 red and green	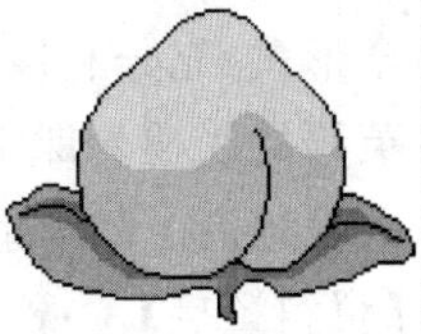 pink
grapes	watermelon	lychee	strawberry	a peach

T：What's this?

Ss：It's an apple. (pear/orange /banana/ ball…)

T：What color is it?

Ss：It's red.（green/orange/yellow/brown…）

2. 学生通过网络资源自主学习颜色单词。

3. 教师帮助学生正音，如教师指着大象图：

T：What's this?

Ss：It's an elephant.

T：What color is it?

Ss：It's grey.

学生跟读几遍后，教师可指着教室里的灯、黑板、门等：

T：What color is the light/board/door?

Ss：It's white/ black/grey.

Step 4：Practive

1. 教师让全班看图造句。

S1：The elephant is grey.

S2：The panda is blank and white.

S3：The lion is brown and yellow.

S4：The giraffe is brown and white.

S5：The monkey is brown and pink.

2. 让两个学习好的学生试着介绍一下某个动物的名称和特征。

T：Peter, can you say something about a panda?

P：OK. Look at the panda. It's big. It's fat. It's black and white. It's very cute. I like it.

…

Step 5：Self-learning

1. 学生看自己电脑里的 rhyme 进行自主学习，然后教师把动物图片一反一正地放在黑板上，让一个小组问一个小组回答，看见动物图的就回答："Yes, I can." 看不见动物图的则答："No, I can't."

2. 学生自主学习故事，并在老师的指导下分成小组表演故事。

【活动评述】

在本设计中，师生打破传统单词教学中单一跟读的教学模式，注重词句相结合的教学形式，充分利用网络资源里图文声并茂、多姿多彩的学习内容，大大激发了学生学习英语的兴趣。课堂上，学生们有了更大的发挥空间，他们主动、互助地学习，帮助教师极大地提高了教学的效率。

【资料链接】

www. xingzhitang. com

（深圳市南山区南山小学　苏凯如）

Birthday Party (2)

【设计理念】

1. 任务驱动，引发学生听读的兴趣。

2. 整体感知，培养学生思维的灵活性和概括性。

3. 分组派对，寓教于乐。

【活动目标】

1. 通过“电话约请朋友”“收、送生日礼物”“开生日会”等活动，提高学生语言应变能力、口语交际能力和运用英语进行思维的能力。

2. 在派对活动中培养孩子文明有礼的语言和行为习惯。

3. 在派对活动中培养孩子们的集体意识。

【活动准备】

1. 网络教室及网页型课件。

2. 与生日会相关的动画故事。

3. 开生日派对用的物品：纸帽子、自制生日贺卡、礼物等。（学生准备）

【活动过程】

1. 任务驱动，阅读对话

T: I know you all like birthday party. Because on your birthday, you can get many presents, you can have a big dinner, and you can play with your friends. Today, we'll learn to hold an English birthday party. OK? You must talk in English, sing in English and play in English. But how to hold a birthday party? Don't worry. I've prepared three dialogues for you. Dialogue 1 will tell you how to invite your friends on the phone. Dialogue 2 will tell you how to give and get presents. Dialogue 3 will tell you some key words for the party. Now, please read the three dialogues by yourselves.

Dialogue 1

Lily: David, please.

David: This is he. Who's that?

Lily: Hi, David. This is Lily. Today is my birthday. Please come to my birthday party this evening.

David: Good! See you then.

Dialogue 2

David: Happy birthday, Lily. This present is for you.

Lily: A doll! How pretty it is! Thank you very much.

David: You're welcome.

Dialogue 3

Lily: It's time to cut cake.

Mum: Let's light the candles.

Dad: Let's sing Happy Birthday song.

Whole: Happy birthday to you…

2. 环环相扣，两两操练

T: I've read the three dialogues, too. Now I know how to invite my friends on the phone. Listen to me, please. Today is my birthday. I am going to hold a birthday party. Now I'll invite my friend, Kitty.

在学生听读后，教师邀请两位同学做示范，进行电话约请、收送礼物、生日活动等外语，然后让学生进行两两练习。教师及时将所学的内容进行巩固和迁移，有利于提高学生运用知识的灵活性。

3. 阅读故事，整体感知

T: Now, you know how to invite your friends, how to give and get presents and how to hold a birthday party. I've prepared some stories about birthday party for you to read. Please choose one.

如果说学生在学完对话后对生日会的感知是片段性的话，那么通过阅读与生日会相关的动画故事后，他们对生日会则会有一个全方位的感受。这一环节的设置有利于培养学生的思维发散性和概括性。

4. 分组派对，快乐实践

T: Now, suppose today is your group leader's birthday. Please hold a birthday party in groups.

学生通过对话、故事的学习，对生日会有了一个清晰的认识。教师在此让学生戴上课前准备的帽子和礼物，开开心心地开一个生日会，是对知识的巩固和提升，也是寓教于乐的体现。轻松的环境更有利于学生无拘无束地交流。

【活动评述】

该教学活动以开生日会为中心任务，为了完成这个任务，教师将课文内容整合、编排成"电话邀请朋友""收送生日礼物""开生日会"三个对话，并准备了一些有关生日会的动画故事，先让学生进行自主阅读，然后邀请学生进行对话示范，再让学生进行两两操练，最后让学生分组开生日会，可谓环环相扣，层层叠进。

【资料链接】

1. 杨开城，李文光，《现代教学设计的理论体系构想》，教育研究，2001

2. 严旭峰，林祖荣，《素质教育下课堂教学设计的新观念》，天津教研网，2003

（深圳市南山区向南小学　覃贵双）

Colors (1)

【设计理念】

怎样才能让全体学生主动、积极、愉悦地说英语呢？我在设计这节课时，在教学目标上，力求以课本为中心，源于教材，但超于教材，尽量挖掘学生的潜能；在教学方法和活动方式的设计上，掌握低龄孩子的心理特点，力求以兴趣、活动、情景为中心，注意孩子们兴趣的同时，也注重课堂的真实性和交际性；在教学涵盖面上，以全体学生为主体，力求让每个同学都愿意开口说。

【活动目标】

1. 学生进一步熟悉和掌握各种颜色的表达方法。

2. 学生学习和掌握下列句型：

What color is it ?

It's…

I like red/ green…

3. 学生能对物体的颜色进行简单的描述。

【活动准备】

1. 学生穿上自己漂亮的衣服。

2.《丑小鸭》英语故事书、音乐伴奏带、教学软件、词卡、画卡、彩笔、纸张、鼓、彩色脚印纸、交通灯卡纸等。

【活动过程】

Step 1：Warm-up

1. Appreciation ：An ugly duckling（配乐，老师带学生一起朗诵）。

2. Sing a song ：What's This in My Classroom? 复习“It's…” 句型。

Step 2：Revision

用颜色卡复习上一节课的内容：brown，red，orange，yellow，green，blue，pink，purple，black，grey，white 等单词和 This is blue /read… 句型。

Step 3：Presentation

1. 教师播放英语教学软件 Beautiful Spring 片段，在情景中呈现重点句型，让学生感受颜色的描述方法。

Hello，Tony! Hello，Jenny!

Hello，Gogo! Hi! Gogo!

What color is this?

It's green.

This is grass. It's green.

What color is this，Tony?

Oh! Gogo! It's red.

This is a flower. It's red.

What color is this?

Oh，Gogo! It's blue.

This is yellow.

Wow!

The flower is blue.

Oops!

This flower is red.

That flower is yellow.

What color is this，Tony?

It's brown.

Thank you，Gogo.

2. 学生看完片段后，教师进行提问。

T：Do you like spring?

Ss：Yes.

T：Sping is coming. It's a colorful world. Beautiful flowers，green trees，lovely birds. Let's make a beautiful spring，ok?

教师出示剪好的卡纸小树，并板书。

T：What's this?

Ss：It's a tree.

T：What color is it?

Ss：It's green.

T：I like green.

教师接着出示红的花、蓝的鸟、绿的草，从而完成句型的导入，并拼出一幅靓丽的春天图。

3. 教师带读句型并做颜色替换练习。

Step 4：Practice and Consolidation

1. 学生谈谈自己和班里同学的穿着颜色。

T：Hi，You are very beautiful today！Your sweater is beautiful，What colour is it?

S1：It's pink.

T：What colour do you like?

S1：I like…

T：Your coat is beautiful！What colour is it?

S2：It's red.

T：What colour do you like?

S2：I like…

教师提问后，小组内讨论成员的穿着颜色。

2. 师生一起玩游戏。

(1) 魔幻花朵

教师准备各种颜色的卡纸，用相同大的卡纸镂空一朵美丽的花朵，把镂花的卡纸放在前面，变化后面的卡纸，使花不断变化着颜色。

T：Let's play a guessing game Magic Flowers. You can guess what colour the flower is? Is it red? Is it blue?

让一个同学(S2)拿着这朵会变颜色的花背向大家，请其他同学问：

S1：Is it green?

S2：Yes，it is. / No，it isn't.

直到猜对，后换另一张卡纸，继续猜。

(2) 踩脚印

教师把各色脚印纸不规则地贴在活动中心的空地上，请一位学生敲鼓点，另一位学生随着鼓点踩着脚印跑，鼓点停则停，然后其他同学齐声问他(她)踩到的脚印："What colour is it?" 回答完毕后，继续敲鼓、踩点。

3. 学生分组画多彩的图画并进行简单的描述。

每小组发一大张白纸，教师给出几类主题(主题以前面学过的单词为主)，如水果屋、学习用品屋、娃娃屋、交通工具屋，每小组任选一个主题，用彩笔合作画画，然后分小组上台展示并做简单的描述，如：This is… / I like…

Step 5：Extension

教师出示三张圆型卡纸作为交通红、黄、绿灯，请一个同学当交警，一个同学当司机，其他人当乘客，玩过马路的游戏，师生一起唱下面的儿歌：

Red light, red light,
stop, stop, stop.
Yellow light, yellow light,
wait, wait, wait.
Green light, green light,
go, go, go.

在游戏中，让学生加强遵守交通规则的认识。

【活动评述】

我们充分考虑小学一年级孩子的心理特点，设计了他们非常喜爱的故事、歌曲、游戏、竞赛、画画、儿歌等活动。这些有趣的、有意义的教学活动，调动了学生的学习积极性，发展了学生的创造性。学生在活动中，运用自己的观察力、想像力、审美力和合作精神进行了主动地学习。

【资料连接】

1. 《丑小鸭》英语故事书选自《幼儿英语》，海天出版社

2. 洪恩英语教学软件

（深圳市南山区海滨小学　汤　静）

Healthy Eating

【设计理念】

利用任务型教学模式，给学生创设一种和谐愉悦的课堂氛围，充分发挥学生的主体性。学生通过的自主学习、互助协作，获得创新思维的发展。

【活动目标】

1. 学生学习饮食方面的可数名词和不可数名词。

2. 学生通过活动了解健康的饮食习惯的重要性。

【活动准备】

1. 教师课前准备四张图片，并通过电脑展示一些图片。

2. 教师给每个同学发一张 A3 纸和一张调查表。

【活动过程】

1. 脑风暴活动：用"What would you like to eat?""What would you like to drink?"等句型，复习学过的可数名词和不可数名词。

2. 给学生展示一个小男孩饮食习惯的图片，让学生以小组的形式进行讨论：什么样的饮食才是健康的饮食。The boy is eating too many sweets and too much meat. Does the boy have unhealthy eating habits?

3. 学生紧紧围绕"What are healthy eating habits?""Keeping good healthy eating is very important."等话题，展开小组讨论。

4. 教师给出一个三角形的表格，向学生提问，为什么我们的健康饮食结构是呈三角形的？让学生分小组展开辩论。每组由两名记录员和三名辩手组成。各组把设计的合理饮食结构图展示在黑板上。最后老师展出最合理的饮食结构图（通过电脑展示）。

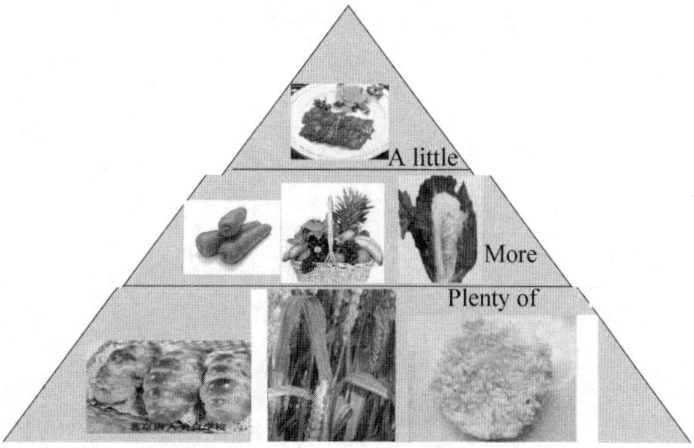

5. 学生做调查活动。教师把事先准备好的调查表发给每个学生，调查的内容是学生在生活中天天接触到的。

Make a survey：Interview one of your classmates.

How much of this food do you eat?

Food	Plenty of /a lot of	A little / a few	I don't eat it /them
Bread and Rice			
Vegetables			
Fruit			
Meat			
Sweets			

Report the results：

My friend A has healthy/ unhealthy eating habits.

…

6. 教师小结：为提高我们自身的体质，从小我们就应该养成良好的饮食习惯。

7. 活动最后以一曲健康歌结束。

【活动评述】

本设计以词汇和句型教学为重点，采用了任务型教学模式。利用生动的语言材料或多样的教学形式不断刺激、提高和保持学生的学习兴趣，寓教于乐。

【资料链接】

1. Integrated Primary English，香港朗文公司，2002

2.《英语课程标准(实验稿)》，北京师范大学出版社，2001

(深圳市南山外国语学校　黄北玲)

A Good Habit

【设计理念】

基于小学生的年龄特征及新课程标准的要求，本设计努力为学生创设活动情境，诱发学生的好奇心。我们充分利用任务型教学模式，通过感知、体验、实践、参与和合作等方式，实现学习任务的目标，让学生感受成功，并促进语言实际运用能力的提高。

【活动目标】

学生能够将句型"How often…?"灵活运用到实际的语言环境中，做到学以致用。

【活动准备】

1. 两张图片：一张为 clean boy A，一张为 dirty boy A。
2. 三张有关学生不良行为习惯的照片。
3. 采访表（每个同学一份）。

【活动过程】

1. 教师以"Keeping clean and tidy is a good habit"为话题，请同学介绍自己的卫生习惯。

2. 教师向学生展示 dirty boy A 的图片，请学生猜：How often does he wash his face/brush his teeth… 最后展示答案。

3. 请学生就 dirty boy 的图片讨论如何使其变成一个 clean boy。例如：He should wash his face every day/ twice a day。教师最后向学生展示 clean boy A 的图片。

4. 教师把事先准备好的采访表发给每个学生，为扩大学生的知识面，所采访的内容应该是学生所感兴趣的，并与实际生活息息相关的。

Interview one of your friends.

Question：How often do you…

采访内容	A day	A week	A month	Optional answers
Have your hair cut				
Watch TV				
Play computer games				
Go to KFC or McDonald's				

Report the result:

My friend B has his/her hair cut once a month, watches TV…

教师要给学生充分的自主权和选择权，让学生在采访内容一列的空格下填上自己想要采访的其他内容。在学生采访之前，教师一定要做清楚的示范。

5. 整个采访及汇报活动结束后，教师即可把话题引入学生日常的行为习惯上，随后展示事先准备好的一些不良行为习惯的图片。请学生以小组的形式讨论并列出日常生活中可见的不良行为习惯。

教师引导小组内成员分工合作，各尽所能。一个记录员，一或二名汇报员，二或三名表演者。当其中一组展示时，其他组要认真观看并删除自己组所列举的相同内容。

6. 请学生自己总结学习内容后，教师进行小结：Everybody should keep good habits all the time and everywhere。并以此为题设计一张宣传画，使活动不局限于课堂，而是延伸到课堂之外的学习和生活中。

7. 最后以一曲图文并茂的 School Rules 歌曲结束。

【活动评述】

本活动以句型教学为重点，采用了任务教学模式。整个教学活动紧紧围绕句型与话题展开，逐步延伸，贴进学生的现实生活，具有一定的可操作性。

但是，要想让学生把每一项任务完成好，教师一定要形成一套有效的控制与协调的方法。首先，学生要熟悉活动模式；组内各成员相对固定，差异互补；全班各小组水平大体均衡。其次，小组目标明确，机会均等。最后，为确保小组活动语言环境的相对真实性，学生一定要有良好的说英语的习惯，这一点要在小组评价与奖励机制中占较大的比例。

【资料链接】

1. Integrated Primary English，香港朗文公司，2002

2.《英语课程标准（实验稿）》，北京师范大学出版社，2001

（深圳市南山外国语学校　王　翔）

Our Fashion Show (3)

【设计理念】

本活动设计遵循“突出学生主体，尊重个体差异”和“采用活动的途径，倡导体验和参与”的新课程理念，采用任务型教学活动模式，力求让学生在活动过程中提高语言运用能力。

【活动目标】

1. 学习 jeans，shorts，shoes，a sweater，socks，trousers 等单词。

2. 学习句型：who is wearing the pink dress? 促进学生学习方式的转变，提高其学习英语的兴趣。

【活动准备】

1. 教师准备 CAI 课件、单词卡片和作为奖品的小卡片。

2. 学生准备剪刀、胶带和各种颜色的彩纸、彩笔。

【活动过程】

Step 1：Look and Say

1. 师生一起唱歌曲 Colours。

2. 展示 CAI 课件，让学生说出各件衣物的名称和颜色以及穿着这些衣服的人物，借此导入句型：Who is wearing the pink dress?

T：What is it?

Ss：It's a sweater.

T：What colour is it?

Ss：It's yellow.

T：Is Tom wearing the yellow sweater?

Ss：Yes，he is. / No，he isn't. Pat is wearing the yellow sweater.

T：Now. Can you tell me who is wearing the yellow sweater?

Ss：Tom is. / Tom is wearing the yellow sweater.

教师让学生互相问答，表现出色的给予奖励。奖品是不同衣物形状的小卡片，上面写着 great、very good、excellent、smart、clever 等单词。

Step 2：Game

教师展示课件，课件中的人物都是学生熟悉的同学和老师，他们都通过了 photoshop 的特效处理，学生只能看到他们的衣着。教师要求学生说出他们穿的是什么，并猜出都是谁。例如：

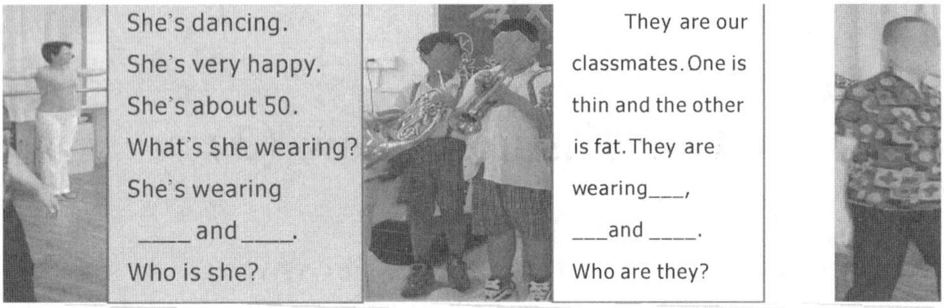

Step 3：DIY

学生以小组为单位(每个小组六个人)，设计自己喜欢的颜色和款式的衣物。教师要求每小组不少于四件自制的衣物模型，并在每件衣物上用不同的英语字体表示出它们的名称，使设计出来的衣物比较有英语的特色。

Step 4：Fashion Show

1. 教师调整学生的座位，使教室中间成 T 型台状。

2. 学生在老师的带领下齐唱歌曲 Tim Is Wearing Black Trousers。

3. 老师任意出示一张单词卡片，改编歌曲中的衣物名称和颜色，与学生一起边打拍子边唱。

例如：Who is wearing blue socks? Blue socks? Blue socks?

4. 每个小组里有这种穿着的学生就出场，走着模特步并响亮地唱道：

I am wearing blue socks. Blue socks. Blue socks today.

5. 如此反复三次，学生就熟悉了游戏的规则。教师让两个学生当主持人，扮演自己的角色。

6. 教师评出表演出色的小组并给予奖励。

【活动评述】

在这个活动中，教师引导学生自己进行服装设计和表演。教师把学生熟悉的事物引入活动，为英语学习创设情景、营造气氛，充分调动学生的积极性，使学生在活动情景中自然地进入学习的状态，在有效的学习方式中完成学习任务。教师鼓励学生积极参与，表现自我，体验成功，让学生充分发挥主体作用。同时，活动还锻炼了学生的动手能力、分析能力、合作能力、审美能力以及交际能力。

【资料链接】

1. http：//www. xinzhitang. com. cn

2. Our fashion show, Book 5, *Primary English for China*

（深圳市南山区大新小学　王幼娟）

Good Manners

【设计理念】

英语是一门实践课,英语学习的首要任务是"学"而不是"教"。我们通过开展情景表演等任务型活动来激发学生对英语学习的探究精神和进行语言实践的热情,锻炼学生收集、组织、传递语言信息的能力,让学生学会"用英语做事",从而提高实际运用语言的能力。

【活动目标】

1. 学生能运用所学句型"You /We/He should…""You/We shouldn't…"进行扩展性的情景会话。

2. 通过小组活动,讨论各场合人们该做和不该做的事,培养学生的文明意识。

3. 通过自编短剧,以小组形式进行争做"Model Student"的汇报表演,培养学生的语言口头表达能力和团结协作精神。

【活动准备】

1. 关于学校、图书馆、公园、影院、医院、家庭等场景的图片和影片。

2. 单词卡(配图):good manners, model student, polite, rude, noisy, rubbish, quiet, corridor, note, signs, rule 等单词及相关句子。

3. 相关的课件。

4. 小组评比使用的奖章。

5. 表演用的道具、服装。

【活动过程】

Step 1:Warm-up

Listen and chant with pictures on the screen.

教师通过 chant 这一热身活动,引导学生复习 good manners 的内容。随着图片及字幕的播放,全体学生边 chant 边拍手,很快能进入英语学习的环境。

Step 2:Revision

Free talk: Revise the words and expression about good manners with word cards and sentence strips.

T: Boys and girls, can you tell me something about good manners? (What are good manners?)Please show me your ideas one by one.

The teacher helps the students by showing them the word cards with pictures.

S1: Walk in the corridor. / We should walk in the corridor.

T：Good. Next one, please.

S2：Don't run in the corridor. / We shouldn't run in the corridor.

T：Well done. Next one, go on please.

S3：Be quiet in the classroom. / We should be quiet in the classroom.

S4：Don't be noisy in the classroom. / We shouldn't be noisy in the classroom.

S5：Don't throw rubbish on the floor. / We shouldn't throw rubbish on the floor.

S6：Be polite.

S7：Don't be rude.

T：Pretty well. You all know what are good manners and what are bad manners. Now let's do some activities. I believe all of you will like to do it.

教师通过以 Free talk 方式描述什么是 good manners 行为，激励学生在图片的帮助下练说句型：We /You should ______. We /You shouldn't ________.

Step 3：Presentation

T：Boys and girls, do you want to be model students? What should we do and what shouldn't we do in these places：(1) At the library；(2) In the park；(3) At home；(4) At the cinema；(5) At school；(6) In the hospital? Ok, let's divide our class into four groups and have a discussion.

Now please watch these programs and comment on these people's behaviors. Then you can make some short stories about manners according to these short films/ pictures and role-play. I hope to see your wonderful manner show. Would you like to do it?

Ss：Sure. We like performance very much.

T：Let's see the short films and discuss in groups.

师生平等交流，由看影片导出思考：What do you think of these people? 影片中各种人物的行为举止引发学生的好奇心，促使学生从无意注意转为有意注意。教师顺势让学生用句型"He should / shouldn't…"分组自由讨论，评议影片中人物的行为举止是否文明。影片中的生活情景引发了学生说的欲望，也为以后的表演做好了铺垫。

Step 4：Preparation

Each group chooses one of the above topics and makes a story about it. During ten minutes' practice, they can take turns to role-play their story in front of the class. The teacher helps them with pictures and key words on the board. The key words may be：

In the park (Picture 1)：pick flowers, climb the tree, fish, walk on the grass, shoot the birds, take photos, sing and dance, etc.

At home (Picture 2)：make a noise, jump and run on the sofas, spill milk on the table, help mother cook, watch TV, read and write, do housework, etc.

At the cinema (Picture 3)：smoke, talk loudly, eat food, enjoy the film, throw rubbish on the floor, etc.

At school (Picture 4): keep quiet, keep clean, draw/ write on the wall, help teachers, help others, be polite/ rude, walk/ run in the corridors, play basketball in the classroom, put the feet on the seat, put the hands into the rubbish bin, etc.

鲜艳有趣的图片、简单明了的词语，给予了学生足够创造和想像的空间，同时也降低了他们语言表达的难度。浓郁的生活情景让学生感到真实、亲切，有话可说、有戏可演。学生们先看图说话，并用上教师所提供的词语，然后由组长分配角色，练习表演。

Step 5: Performance

T: I know you have special talents in performance. Are you ready to show here? Come on, please.

The children role-play their stories group by group. The stories may be:

Group 1

Ss(Group 1) : Our story is about Mark's happy day. It happens in Zhongshan Park.

Mark : Today is Sunday. Mum, are you free? Sister and I want to play in Zhongshan Park. Would you like to go with us?

Mum : Ok, let's go.

Narrator : Mark and his family are taking photos in the park. They are very happy. Suddenly, Mark sees some people are doing bad things. He tries to stop them.

Tom : How beautiful the flowers are! Let me pick some for you, Mary. (Tom picks the flowers for Mary)

Mark : You shouldn't pick flowers, Sir. It's bad manner. (Mark shows the sign Don't pick flowers! to Tom)

Tom : I'm Sorry.

John : Look! Jim. There are some eggs in the tree. Let's fetch them. (They climb up the tree to fetch the eggs)

Mark : You shouldn't climb the tree. It's dangerous. (Use body language to stop them)

John/Jim : Sorry.

Bill : Oh, how fat the bird is! It's delicious for dinner. (Bill looks happy and shoots at the bird with a gun)

Mark : You shouldn't kill the bird! Animals are our friends. We should protect them.

Bill : I'm very sorry. I won't do it again. (He looks shame)

Jack : Oh, there are many fishes here. Let's fish. (Pretend to fish)

Mark : You shouldn't fish here. (Point to the sign "No fishing"and stop Jack)

Jack: I'm sorry.

Group 2

Ss(Group 2): At the cinema, the people are enjoying the film. Suddenly, some people rush into the cinema. What happens? Please look at our show.

Ken/Tim/Dick: Get away. They are our seats. You shouldn't take our seats. (The three boys are late. They rush into the cinema, with cigarettes in their mouths and food in their hands. They smoke, eat food, and talk loudly)

S1: You shouldn't smoke here. (Show them the sign "No smoking")

S2: You shouldn't throw rubbish on the floor. Please put it in the bin. (Point to the rubbish bin and the sign "Keep clean")

S3: You should be quiet / You shouldn't be noisy. (Point to the sign Keep quiet)

Ken/Tim/Dick: It's none of your business!
(Continue to smoke and eat food with noises)

Ss: You are very rude. You can't stay here.

Ken/Tim/Dick: Ha, ha, ha! Nobody can stop us. (They shout and laugh and the people can't suffer from them any more)

Ss: Policeman! There are some rude men here.

Policemen: Stop! You should be polite. Nobody likes rude men.
(The policemen take them away)

Ss: Thank you, Sir.

Policemen: You're welcome.

T: Wonderful ! Do you enjoy their show? Now Group 3 will give us their show.

Group 3

Ss (Group 3): Today is Sunday. Bob is staying at home. What's he doing? Please look.

Mum: Bob, I'm busy, can you help me? (She is cooking)

Bob: No, I can't. I'm watching TV. (He's running and jumping on the sofas)

Sisters: You shouldn't run and jump on the sofa. You should sit on it.

Bob: Yes, Madam. (Make a face)

Mum: Would you like a glass of milk? (Pass him a glass of milk)

Bob: Yes. (He drinks the milk and spills it on the table/ sofas)

Sisters : You shouldn't spill the milk on the table / sofas, naughty boy!

Bob : Oh, I know.

Mum : Clean the table / sofas, Bob.

Bob : No, brothers can do it.

Brothers : You're lazy! Do you want to be a model student?

Bob: Sure!

Brothers: You should help at home.

Brother 1: You should clean the rooms. (Pass him the broom)

Brother 2: You should wash the dishes. (Pass him the brush)

Brother 3: You should make the bed.

Brother 4: You should be polite and helpful to others.

Bob: Ok, I'll try.

Brothers : Good boy!

T: Excellent! Now Group 4, please. Come on, boys and girls. Be confident!

Group 4

Ss (narrator): In the classroom the pupils are having an English lesson. They like English very much.

Small teacher: Boys and girls, let's practise B1 in pairs, please. (The pupils in Group4 begin to make dialogues in pairs)

S1 : I can play now. (He takes out the football and begins to play)

Ss : You shouldn't play football in the classroom.

S2 : I like drawing. (He begins to draw on the desk / wall)

Ss : You shouldn't draw on the wall. You should draw on the paper after class.

S3 : Miss X, can I help you? (She wants to help the teacher collect workbooks / clean the board)

Small teacher : Thank you. You are kind.

S4 : I am tired. (He puts the feet on the seat / desk and have a rest)

Ss : You shouldn't put your feet on the seat/ desk. You should put them on the floor.

S4 : I'm sorry.

Small teacher : Now let's sing an English song Please and Thank You. one, two, begin!

Ss : Please and Thank you. Please and Thank you. Three little words, three little words. Make our parents happy, make our parents happy.

Yes, we do. Yes, it's true. (The students sing together)

教师把全班分成四个组，要求每组选一个表演课题，一起排练自编的短剧。学生可参照教师提供的图片和句子/剧本，进行自由发挥。教师看谁具备 Good manners 就给佩戴奖章，反之，Bad manners 的则给黑章。教师到各组去指导排练，同时也可充当某一角色，与学生同台演出。

Step 6: Summary

T: Boys and girls, our manner show is over. Now, can you tell me who are model people in the stories?

Ss: Mark, Bob's sisters…

T: Why?

Ss: Because they are kind, polite and helpful to others. (The teacher show the words and help the students to say)

T: Yes. I believe all of you will be model students if you try your best. But do you know how to be model students? What should we do and what shouldn't we do in our daily life?

Ss: We should/ shouldn't…

学生表演完后，教师评出剧中的 Model Student，再为各组颁发奖品，最后让学生自己总结怎样具备 good manners，怎样成为 Model Student。

【活动评述】

曾经有位美国教育学家写过这样一首诗：

How to teach children?
I tried to teach my child with books,
He only gave me puzzled looks;
I tried to teach my child with woods,
They passed him by, often unheard;
Despairingly, I turned aside,
"How shall I teach this child?"
I cried.
"Come!" said he,
"Play with me!"

"玩"是孩子的天性，情景表演更是他们"玩"的专利。本课教学从激发学生兴趣入手，创设家庭、公园、影院等半虚拟情景，引导学生由词到句、由句到篇，循序渐进地达到教学目标。整个教学过程体现合作探究、全员参与，体现学生自主学习及真实的生活实践，让学生在活动中开始、在情境中操练、在运用中创新，从而有效提高学生的语言应用能力。

【资料链接】

1. http://www.xinzhitang.com
2. 《英语沙龙》

（深圳市南山区大冲小学　吴海英）

Eating Out

【设计理念】

本活动设计遵循“突出学生主体，采用活动途径，倡导体验和参与”的新课程理念，始终以学生为中心，倡导学生的积极参与，让学生在学习过程中提高语言能力。本设计借助游戏，激发学生的兴趣和求知欲望，让学生在活动中自导自演，从而活跃课堂气氛，改变“一本教材，一支粉笔，一讲到底”的陈旧的教学模式。

【活动目标】

1. 学习单词及词组：a sandwich，a hamburger，a packet of fries，a bowl of noodles，a piece of cake，a glass of juice 等。

2. 学习句型：Do you like sandwiches? What would you like? I'd like some hamburgers 等。

【活动准备】

教师和学生分别准备食物及饮料的图片。

【活动过程】

Step 1：Warming-up and Revision

1. Daily English.

2. 教师出示图片(都是学生们爱吃的食物、爱喝的饮料)导入新单词。

Step 2：Practice

1. 游戏：教师把各张食物图片贴在黑板上。

T：What's for dinner?

T：Which is your favourite food?

2. 句型操练：What would you like? I'd like a sandwich 等。

3. Chant：What's for dinner? What's for dinner?
What would you like for dinner?
Hamburgers and sandwiches，hamburgers and sandwiches.
I'd like hamburgers and sandwiches.

4. 教师做动作、说英语，引导学生用接龙的形式进行句型的操练。

T：I'm very hungry. What's for dinner?

Ss：What would you like?

T：I'd like some…

5. Let the students look at the picture, listen to the recording, and say something about it.

让学生带着问题听录音，可以训练学生的听力及运用英语进行思维的能力。让学生描述图片，可以加强学生看图说话的能力。

6. Act the dialogue out. 全班同学共分六组：

第一组同学在快餐厅吃饭。

第二组同学在西餐厅吃饭。

第三组同学和家长、亲戚在酒店吃饭。

第四组同学扮演小动物，参加小白兔的生日派对。

第五组同学正在商场购物，准备参加学校的春游活动。

第六组同学正在 KFC 参加一个同学的生日派对。

角色扮演满足了学生爱表现的欲望，提高了学生的表演才能，同时也使学生们身临其境，体验了西方人的就餐习惯，学生们表演后，教师要及时对他们的表演进行评价，对他们的进步和成绩适时加以肯定，同时对他们一些大胆的、失败的尝试也应给予赞赏和鼓励。

Step 3：Extension and Consolidation

1. 单词滚雪球活动，例如：

What would you like for dinner?

I'd like some rice.

I'd like some rice and chicken.

I'd like some rice, chicken and vegetables.

2. Listen and draw.

听录音前，先让学生猜测图意，有助于培养学生的看图说话能力和拓展学生的发散性思维能力。

3. Homework：

询问家庭成员喜欢吃的食物和喜欢喝的饮料，并改编成对话。

【活动评述】

小学阶段是培养学生学习兴趣的关键时期，所以激发学生参与教学活动的动机和兴趣非常重要。本课的教学活动设计贴近学生生活，符合小学生的年龄特点和认知特征，为学生创设真实的语言环境，通过做游戏、唱歌、会话表演等活动，调动了学生学习的积极性，发挥了学生的主体作用。

【资料链接】

1.《英语课程标准(实验稿)》，北京师范大学出版社，2001 年

2. Eating out, Book 3, *Primary English for China*

（深圳市南山区南油小学　吴　莹）

Senses

【设计理念】

教师应以多元、多维的视觉看待学生的智能，拓展教学思维和手段，促使学生的全面发展。本课教学活动设计，以培养学生的英语语言智能为重点，创设情景，鼓励学生积极参与课堂实践活动，培养学生的自主、探究、合作和创新的精神。

【活动目标】

1. 学习交通工具类的七个新单词。
2. 学习并运用新句型进行扩展性的情景会话。

【活动准备】

1. 多媒体课件。
2. 单词卡、图片、各式交通工具的玩具、橙子、香蕉、蛋糕等。

【活动过程】

Step 1：Warm-up and Revision

1. Greetings.
2. Sing a song.

   Head，Shoulders，Knees and Toes.

   （老师带领学生一边唱歌一边表演）
3. Say a chant.

   How do you，how do you come to School?

   By bus/bike/taxi/minibus…

   （教师带领学生把过去所学过的交通工具说一遍）
4. Free talk.

小结：自然、亲切的师生问候揭开活动的序幕；唱歌和表演调动起学生的积极性，激发起学生的学习兴趣；自由对话又给学生营造很好的用英语进行交流的机会。整个活动既是热身，又活跃了课堂气氛；同时也复习了旧知识，为学习新课做下铺垫。

Step 2：Presentation and Practice

1. 播放 CD，让学生感受情景，理解内容。

T：What can you see?

Ss：I can see a plane. I can see…

2. 教授新内容：

(1) 教师播放自制的课件。首先屏幕上出现一个长方形,教师问学生:“What's this?”启发学生想像。接着,屏幕上出现的一个又一个的长方形慢慢聚拢、渐变,到许多零部件的图组合成交通工具图时,教师出示新单词,并引导学生进行看图、听音、跟读、个人读、小组内交流读等活动。最后教师教授新单词:a train, a plane, a van, a road, a lorry, a ship, a truck 等。

(2) 把学生分成七组,每组学生代表一种交通工具。如 Group Train, Group Van 等。每组推选一个学生上台扮演交通工具。

T: You are a train. Mr Train, welcome!

S1: I'm a train. I'm Mr Train.

上台的学生举起手中的交通工具图片并做自我介绍,七个“交通工具”一个接一个地介绍并互相问候。

S2: Good morning, Mr Train.

S3: How are you, Miss Ship?

小结:活动根据儿童的心理特征,在课堂上设计一些悬念,利用小学生想知道答案的心情,引发学生对答案的探究和思考。游戏和表演激发了学生的学习欲望,激活了学生的想像力。活动既巩固了新单词,又培养了学生说英语的能力。

3. 教师根据本课的教学目标,设计三个问题。

(1) What can you see?

(2) What can you see in the classroom?

(3) What can you do with your eyes/ears/nose?

4. 根据问题,引导学生观察周围环境。

T: Please tell me what you can see in this classroom.

Ss: I can see a blackboard / desk…

T: I see with my eyes. I can see Peter. 老师指着自己的眼睛说,而学生模仿着说,并根据情景进行对话。教师点击鼠标,屏幕上出现了卡通图案的各种交通工具后,引导学生进行描述。

T: Listen! Can you tell me what you can hear?

Ss: I can hear a car…

T: OK! I can hear a car. I hear with my ears.

老师拿出预先准备好的橙子、蛋糕、香蕉等食品,引导学生进行观察。

T: Can you see an orange?

Ss: Yes.

T: I can smell an orange.(老师一边切开橙子一边面带表情地说)

5. Practice in pairs.

学生拿出准备好的图片、玩具车、食物等,分组进行情景会话。

小结:学习英语的目的是为了在合适的情景中运用。创设情景能使学生置身语言情景中,把呆板的知识转化为活的语言,从而增强对语言的理解力及交流运用的能力。

Step 3: Game

教师播放“Listen and Guess”的多媒体课件,让大家推荐一名小主持人。主持人点击鼠标，屏幕上出现了一组五个并排的正方形，每个正方形代表一种交通工具。主持人点击任意一个正方形，就发出一种交通工具的声音。教师组织学生猜，看谁最先说出相对应的单词。猜对了的话，正方形的下面就会跳出此单词并发出声音。教师提问："What can you see? What can you hear?"主持人点击另一组正方形，每一个正方形代表一种食物。教师接着提问："What can you smell?"全班分成七个小组，举手进行抢答，教师给猜对的组加分奖励。

小结：活动把竞争引入课堂，给学生开放的思维空间，让其在听一听、猜一猜、玩一玩的过程中学到知识，既活跃了课堂气氛，调动了学生的积极性，又达到了在轻松愉快的氛围中巩固单词知识的目的。

Step 4：Song

教师播放课件，屏幕上出现配乐图片。

I can see a ______ with my eyes. 

I can hear a ______ with my ears. 

I can smell a ______ with my nose. 

学生跟唱，并根据图唱出所缺的词。活动在欢快的歌声中结束。

小结：活动始终体现"以学生为主体"的原则，体现以培养学生兴趣和传授知识相结合的原则。

Step 5：Homework

Making sentences about some of the objects at home.

【活动评述】

教师是否具有新课程的教学理念，是新课程改革能否成功的关键。在本课的教学活动设计中，教师以学生为本，借鉴多元智能理论，以多元、多维的全新视野，促使学生的知识和能力、方法和技能、情感态度和价值观这三维目标的整合，并充分运用英语课的特点，把教学资源、信息技术手段与课程相整合。

【资料链接】

1.《英语课程标准(实验稿)》，北京师范大学出版社，2001 年

2. Senses, Book 4, *Primary English for China*

(深圳市南山区南头城小学　徐丽嘉)

Colors (2)

【设计理念】

基础教育阶段英语教学的主要目的在于激发学生的学习兴趣和培养学生良好的学习习惯。对于低年段的英语教学来说，培养听、说能力尤其重要。英语教学中的“说”包含了两个方面：一是朗读的能力，即学生跟读课文，模仿读音或经过学习后自己能朗诵课文的能力；二是说话的能力，即学生把从课本中所学的知识，经过内部消化，再用自己的方式表达出来，与他人进行沟通和交流的能力，这也是我们英语学习的最终目的。在本设计活动中，我们根据学生的特点，设计了适合他们的游戏活动，让学生在游戏活动中主动积极地与他人交流，大胆地“说”英语。

【活动目标】

1. 学生能在真实自然的环境中熟练询问和回答各种有关颜色的问题，并能区分“What color is the… It's… ”“What color are the… They are…”等单复数句型。

2. 学生通过寻找和讨论春天的各种颜色，认识到春天的美丽和可爱。

【活动准备】

1. 学生熟知有关颜色的单词，如 black, orange, grey, white, purple, pink 等。

2. 学生初步掌握单复数 is 和 are 及 it 和 they 的区别，并能用有关知识进行问答。

3. 教师准备两组相同的有关春天的图画，但分别在不同的地方涂上颜色。

4. 照相机。

【活动过程】

1. 两两对话，涂涂画画

为了激发学生学习英语的兴趣，促使他们在创设的语言环境中，积极主动地开口“说”，教师安排两个学生为一组，每人手中都有一幅相同但分别在不同地方已经涂上颜色的图画。同组的两个学生不能看对方手里的图画，他们必须通过问答来获得自己想要的信息。比如，一个学生询问：“What color is the bird?”另一个学生看着自己的图画回答：“It's pink.”然后再反问自己的伙伴：“What color are the flowers?”他的伙伴又根据自己的图画颜色回答：“They're red and yellow.”就这样，两两学生必须团结合作，互相询问对方有关自己图画的颜色。涂完颜色后，教师再让同组的学生互相对比对方手里的图画，检查自己的学习成果。

2. 互相展示，你问我答

教师打开投影机，让同组的学生拿着各自的图画进行展示，同时进行简单的、有关图画的对话。例如，学生甲询问："What color is the house?"学生乙熟练地回答："It is blue."然后他再反问："What color are the grasses?"学生甲指着自己的图画大声地回答：They are green.

3. 校园景色，五彩缤纷

最后为了进一步训练学生的口语交际能力，激发他们自主说英语的积极性，教师带领学生走出课堂，到校园的各个角落去寻找春天的颜色。在这不受约束的空间里，学生没有任何的心理负担，他们兴高采烈地看着周围的秀丽景色，用课堂上所学的知识大胆地相互询问、相互学习。例如：

S1：Look at the tree, what color is it?

S2：It's green.

S3：What color are the grasses?

S4：They're green, too.

S5：What color is the butterfly?

S6：It's yellow and black.

教师在旁边做指导，及时解决学生不懂的问题，比如教他们说一些没有接触过的单词和句子。此外，教师可以鼓励学生在谈论过程中用照相机把自己喜欢的景色拍下来，从而加深对春天颜色的了解。

【活动评述】

在教师的带领下，孩子们兴高采烈地走出了教室，在学校的各个角落，用英语兴奋、自由、欢快地交流着。从孩子们欢乐的笑脸，我们看到了最美的春天，也感受到了课改在师生教学互动中所带来的巨大改变。新课程、新目标赋予了我们新的观念、新的教法，我们不再局限于旧的、单一的传统教学模式。我们可以根据实际需要、学生状况及身边的环境，灵活地应用教学方法和教学模式，帮助学生更好地发展和学习。

【资料链接】

1. 强海燕，《幼儿英语浸入式教育活动》，西安交通大学出版社，2000

2. Sarsh，《牛津英语教师宝库》，华东师范大学出版社，牛津大学出版社，1999

3. 广东外国语师范学校，《齐齐学英语》，广东人民出版社

（中央教育科学研究所南山附属学校　王　华）

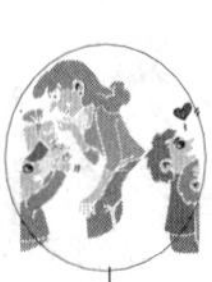

Our Friends

【设计理念】

我们运用现代技术搜集和处理信息，以教材为基础，并活用教材，把英语学习拓展到生活中，让学生自由地去探究、去实践。

【活动目标】

1. 通过游戏活动复习职业单词和相关句型。

2. 学生描述生活中的人物，以达到活学活用的目的。

【活动准备】

录音机、投影仪、图片、电脑及课件。

【活动过程】

1. 师生问候。

2. 热身、布置任务：全班学生边舞边唱歌曲 Two Little Fat Birds，由曲中的 Peter 和 Paul 是好朋友，引出本次活动的主题“Our friends”。然后教师交代本次活动的目标：比谁交的朋友多？比谁能最快用英语描述自己的朋友、同学。

3. 复习职业单词的游戏：请一名学生上来模仿某一职业（如医生）的常见动作，另一名学生用 Is he/ she a doctor/ nurse/ driver/ teacher/ policeman/ policewoman? 来猜测，全班学生作答。

复习 Who's that/ he/ she? 问答句的游戏：一名学生看单词卡后表演动作，全班问：“Who's that/ he/ she?”另一名学生根据前一名学生的动作回答他/她的职业。

这两个环节都是为后面的进一步学习做知识准备的。游戏可以让学生在不知不觉的玩乐中获得必备的知识，游戏还能引起学生浓厚的兴趣和主动的学习欲望。

4. 请一位学生上黑板前蒙住眼睛，用手去触摸另一位学生的五官，然后，猜对方是谁。这对蒙眼的学生有点难度，但猜不中不要紧，因为这只不过是教学活动的一个引子：如果想知道对方是谁，可以通过倾听别人的描述来猜出来。教师自然而然地就可以引出下文：

She's a girl. She has long hair. She has a round face. She's tall. She's a little bit fat. Who's she? Is she a teacher? 此时学生再猜就不难了，教学也自然过渡到下一环节。

5. 学生看电脑显示的三位外貌特征突出的动画人物，听老师描述其中一个人物的外貌，并猜猜：Who's that? 教师的描述如下：

I have a friend. He has a round face. He has two small ears. He has a big mouth. He has short hair. He has a pair of glasses on his nose. He can drive a bus. Who's that?（请一位学生回答，并在电脑上选择、点击相应的人物）学生操作的同时回答教师的问题：What's he? Is he a teacher? 学生根据实际作答：Yes, he is. /No, he isn't. He's a driver.

6. 教师提供一些影视和体育明星的大特写，让学生练习描述和作答。例如：

(1) She's tall. She has big eyes. She has long hair. She can act, sing and dance. She's beautiful. Who's she? What's she? Is she a…

(2) He's tall. He has big eyes. He has short hair. He can play basketball very well. Who's he? What's he? Is he a…

（省略号代表学生可以根据学过的职业单词来猜）

7. 教师设计三个卡通人物让学生学习写描述性的小短文。例如：

(1) He has big eyes. He has a big yellow mouth. He has big hands. He is lovely and wonderful. Who's that? What's he? Is he a…

(2) He has a big mouth. He has black ears. He has a big black nose. He has big feet. He's smart and cute. He's Donald's good friend. Who's that?

(3) He is a superman. He is red. He has big golden eyes. He can fly. He is brave and strong. Who's that?

学生练读这三段小短文，学习其中的新单词。

8. 教师请学生模仿小短文描述一名在座的学生，让其他同伴猜，把所学的知识再次运用到实际的情景中。

9. 老师小结：今天我们认识了很多很多的朋友，大家都很棒！让我们唱一首歌来结束我们的课吧！

【活动评述】

这是一节巩固课，是在学了一些职业单词的基础上拓展、整合的一个课堂教学活动设计。教师考虑到了巩固课活动时间多的特点，让全体学生积极参与，尽量发挥学生的主体性。活动内容的设计富有趣味性，通过创设游戏猜人物复习单词、句型，描述熟悉的老师和明星，让学生把知识点运用到真实的情景中。最后三个卡通人物的学习，也是这节课的主要拓展目标，它是学生由口头对话转入 short introduction passage 的一个桥梁，这有助于让学生把这些知识运用到实际生活中，使所学的语言成为交流的工具。

【资料链接】

1.《英语课程标准(实验稿)》，北京师范大学出版社，2001 年

2. 欧美儿童流行歌曲

（深圳市南山区育才一小　梁淑珍）

I Say,You Guess

【设计理念】

培养低年级学生用英语进行活动和交流的乐趣和兴趣，让学生在参与、合作中体验英语学习的成功与喜悦。

【活动目标】

通过猜谜语、编谜语，巩固所学的颜色、动词、形容词等方面的词汇和相关句型等语言知识，培养学生的观察能力，提高学生学习英语的兴趣。

【活动准备】

各种水果图，各种动物头饰，幻灯片。

【活动过程】

Step 1：Riddles

1. 老师出示各种学生已学过的水果图，学生说出相应水果的英文名称和颜色。

2. 在学习了相关的单词和句型的基础上，老师说一个 riddle 让学生猜，学生猜对后，教师最后做一定的解释。Riddle 如下：

Who am I?
I am round.
I am big.
I am sweet.
I am green outside.
But red inside.
Who am I?

3. 小组活动(老师指导学生，并把相关单词写在黑板上)。

(1) 分组：4～6 人为一小组，也可以根据班里的实际情况进行分组。

(2) 布置任务：学生选一种或几种水果编成 riddle，可以单独编，也可以几人合作。

(3) 学生把编成的 riddle 讲给班上其他小朋友听。

Step 2：Competion

1. 老师出示各种学生已学过的动物头饰，让学生说出相应的英文名称和动物的一些基本特征。

例如：Dog 的一些特征。

It can run very fast.

It likes meat.

It has four legs.

It barks Woo, Woo…

2. 在复习了相关的单词和句型(英文名称和基本特征)后,老师组织小组竞猜活动。

(1) 分组:六人一小组,也可以根据班里的实际情况进行分组。

(2) 活动安排:每一次由一个小组说一个谜语,小组代表轮流说谜语。

每一次从各组中选一个同学到讲台前进行比赛,一次猜一个谜(也可猜两到三个谜语),然后换另一组。

(3) 活动操作:说谜语的同学应一句一句地说,留出适当的时间让同学思考。

每一次允许举手快的同学先作答,答对则加分。或者同学们听完谜语后,把自己的谜底写在小木板或白纸上。

相关练习:可以把谜语拓展到生活用品上。

活动中,把各类型谜语混在一起会更有趣味性和挑战性。

【活动评述】

采用低年级学生喜欢的谜语的形式可以帮助他们巩固学过的语言知识。小朋友在编谜语的过程中会选自己喜欢的、熟悉的一种事物,实现经验向能力的迁移。正如杜威所强调的,学习者要有一种"经验的真实情境",而且在这种情境里面,要有促使学习者去思考的"真实的问题","教学应从学生的经验和活动出发,使学生在游戏和工作中,采用与自己生活接近的活动形式"。

【资料链接】

1.《英语课程标准(实验稿)》,北京师范大学出版社,2001 年

2. 郭元祥,《论教育的生活意义和生活的教育意义》,2003 年 7 月

(深圳市南山区塘朗小学　钟灿权)

I Am a Little Journalist

【设计理念】

1. 从学生的学习兴趣、生活经验和认知水平出发，设计贴近学生生活的交际活动，让学生在活动中通过参与、实践、体验，最终发展综合语言运用的能力。

2. 活动的任务是采访。让学生在完成任务的过程中形成积极的情感与态度，促进语言交流功能的实现。

3. 使英语课堂情景化、生活化、社会化。

【活动目标】

通过采访任务的活动，培养学生用英语收集他人的信息并处理信息的能力。

【活动准备】

三张白纸：两张用于制作话筒，一张用于设计表格、图表等。

【活动过程】

1. 教师把全班分成6～8个组，每组5～6人。活动以小组为单位进行。

2. 教师用两张纸制作成一个记者采访用的话筒：一张制作成一个正立方体，四面写上电视台的字样；另一张制作成话筒。

这一步看似与主题活动无关，但它是顺利、高效地完成任务的工具。英语教学要求创设尽可能逼真的情景，因为真实的场景能激发学生交流的激情与冲动，激发学生的兴趣与参与欲望。当学生拿着自制的话筒得意洋洋、跃跃欲试时，你可以预期：活动已成功了一半。

3. 教师帮助学生设计采访任务。这一环节是开放式的、灵活的，难易度要根据学生的已有水平来确定。低年级学生可以做一些简单的采访和提问，形式可以是表格、图表、信息卡等。高年级学生则可相应地增加信息的容量。

低年级提问方式举例：

Name: ________
Age: ________
Nationality: ________
Class ______, Grade ______
Telephone: ______
E-mail: ________

What's your name?
How old are you?
Where are you from?
What's your telephone/E-mail…
What class are you in?

高年级提问形式参考：

What's your favourite animal/colour/fruit/food/drink/festival…

What subject/sport…do you like best?

How many people are there in your family?

When/where/How often do you play football?

What do you often do after school/at home…

学生可以就某一具体的话题来展开采访，如爱好、行为习惯等，或者把采访范围再细化，如运动爱好、饮食偏好等。但要注意以下几点：

(1) 采访对象最好不要是学生最熟悉的朋友，否则就不能形成最有效的信息沟通。

(2) 表格设计的书写量要少，否则会破坏采访的连贯性。

(3) 教师鼓励基础较好的学生先采访。

4. 教师先找一个学生作为采访对象做一个示范。

5. 每个小组推举一名学生做全班交流，然后选出“最佳小记者”。

【活动评述】

本案例考虑了小学生的认知规律与特点，把小学生的有意识学习与无意识习得有机地结合起来，采用听、做、说、唱、玩、演的方式，以活动为主来开展教学，给学生提供了充分的语言实践机会。通过采访的形式，一些最平常的问句跳出了问句本身的属性，变成了完成任务的交际工具，真正实现了英语的交际功能。

【资料链接】

1. 《英语课程标准(实验稿)》，北京师范大学出版社，2001

2. www.nse.cn

3. www.cbe21.com

（深圳市南山区西丽小学　周明龙）

Where Is the Bookshop

【设计理念】

“任务就是人们在日常生活、工作、娱乐活动中所从事的各种各样的有目的的活动。任务型语言教学的核心思想是要模拟人们在社会、学校生活中运用语言所从事的各类活动，把语言教学与学习者在今后日常生活中的语言应用结合起来。任务型语言教学把人们在社会生活中所做的事情细分为若干非常具体的‘任务’，并把培养学生具备完成这些任务的能力作为教学目标。”（龚亚夫，罗少茜）

【活动目标】

1. 学会问路及给人指路。
2. 通过地图指示建筑物的方位。
3. 向他人介绍自己所居住的社区。

【活动准备】

1. 一张显示学校及其附近标志性建筑物的简单平面地图。
2. 一张仅有街道名称的空白平面地图。

【活动过程】

1. Pre-task preparation

Show the map of the school and the places nearby.

T：(Point to the school and ask) What's this place?

Ss：It's our school, Zhuguang Primary School.

T：Yes. Where's our school?

Ss：It's in Longzhusan Street.

T：Is there a supermarket?

Ss：Yes, there is. It's Vanguard Supermarket.

T：Where is the supermarket?

Ss：It's in Zhuguang Street.

…

通过与学生谈论他们所熟悉的学校及其周围环境，复习已学句型：Is there a… 及相关单词：supermarket，clinic，post office，bookshop，cinema，park 等，并引入“Where's the…”和“It's in…”等目标句型。

2. While-task process

出示一幅标有街道名称的地图，要求学生：① 按自己的设想，在图中的方框处，标上建筑物的名称，并且保密；② 学生两人一组，通过互问互答，完成 My friend's poster，具体如下：

A：Is there a…

B：Yes，there is. / No，there isn't. But there's a…

A：Where's the…

B：It's in… Street.

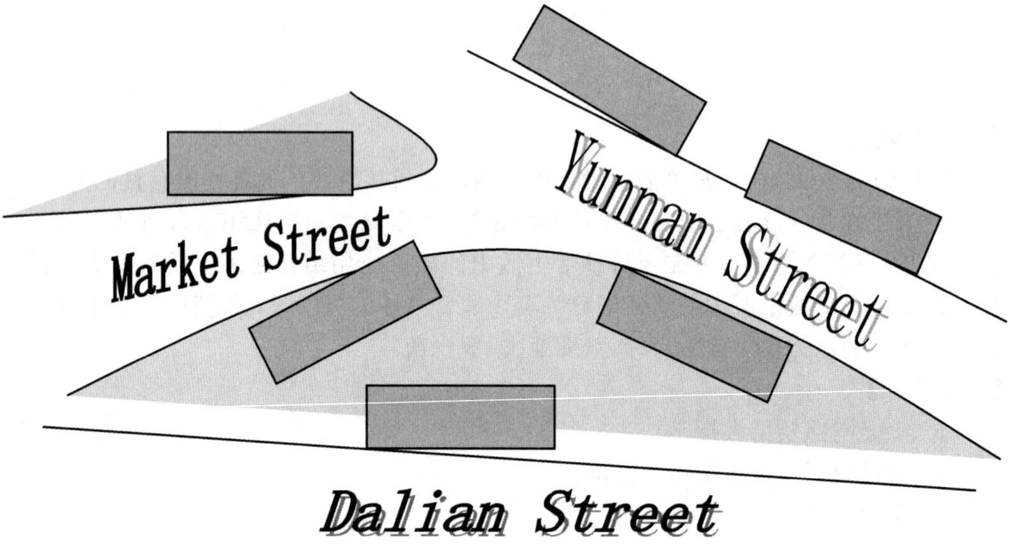

My friend's poster：

Come to City Centre	
There's a ________.	There's a ________.
It's in ________ Street.	It's in ________ Street.
There's a ________.	There's a ________.
It's in ________ Street.	It's in ________ Street.

3. Post-task activity

任务一：请来我家玩

让学生邀请自己的好朋友到家里玩，并且边描述路径，边画一张简单的指路地图，标出相关的标志性建筑。

任务二：问路

受到邀请的同学在前往的路上丢了地图，只能凭记忆问路前去。

【活动评述】

1. 任务型语言教学似乎并不主张让学生在对所谈主题毫无思想准备的情况下，直接接受新的语言材料，而往往注重激活学生已有的生活与学习经验，从学生熟悉的语言材料入手，介绍该语言的使用环境及把与话题有关的思维脉络、思维发散的方向也同时提供给学生。因此，本设计借助学生熟悉的学习生活环境引入话题，使学生学起来自然、流畅。

2. 任务型教学并不排斥句型语法练习，只是要求尽量使这种枯燥的练习变得有意义。因此，我们设计了一个半控制性的有意义练习，让学生练习巩固所学的单词与句子。

3. 任务型语言教学强调用语言做事，强调做中学的过程，强调培养学生语言的运用能力。本设计中两个任务贴近学生生活经验，能使学生学以致用，使其语言的实际运用能力得到锻炼和提高。

【资料链接】

1.《英语课程标准(实验稿)》，北京师范大学出版社，2001

2. 龚亚夫、罗少茜，《任务型语言教学》，人民教育出版社，2003

3. Nunan, D. Designing Tasks for Communicative Classroom，人民教育出版社，2001

（深圳市南山区珠光小学　余林秀）

How to Use a Dictionary

【设计理念】

字典是学习英语的必备工具，英语教师应帮助学生学会使用字典，并培养学生勤查字典的好习惯。本课教学可根据学生的不同年级和不同英语水平而进行相应的调整。

【活动目标】

让学生学会查字典，为今后的学习打下基础。

【活动准备】

学生每人准备一本学生字典（最好是英汉双解的），笔和纸。

【活动过程】

1. 教师先提示学生以下一些查字典的要领，以帮助他们顺利上路。

(1) 熟悉字母的顺序。

字典的字序是按照字母的顺序排列的。学生除了要熟悉 A 到 Z 的顺序外，也要能熟练地由 Z 倒念到 A。教师可请学生做下列的练习。

① 练习将下列单字按照首字母顺序排列：

intensive　mobile　vouch　done　deer　slender

② 练习将下列单字按照字典上出现的顺序排列：

gambit　gamble　gusty　ground　gold　gray

(2) 熟悉字典里各字母开头字汇的位置。

学生查字典前，先让学生熟悉每个字母开头字汇出现的范围。例如：找出以 F 字母开头的字汇出现在字典的范围，并做标示。有些字典会将各字母出现的部分在字典的侧面以区块标出，有些字典则直接标出 A 到 Z，这些标示都能帮助使用者搜寻资料。

(3) 利用引导字(guide word)。

字典的最上方都列有引导字。学生若能有效运用引导字的提示，就能快速翻到生词出现的位置。

(4) 熟悉字典里的符号。

教师可介绍字典里常用的符号，让学生了解符号所代表的意思。例如：

名词	代词	形容词	副词	动词
n.	pron.	adj.	adv.	v.
冠词	介词	连接词	感叹词	
art.	prep.	conj.	interj.	

另外，代表可数名词的 c. 及代表不可数名词的 u. 也是字典里常见的符号。教师可请学生利用字典查出下表中的单词，并以符号写出词性，以加深记忆。

pretty	they	jacket	above	and	the	carefully	act	oh

2. 根据学生所在年级和所学英文程度的不同，教师可配合教学单元进行一些活动，让学生练习搜寻资料，使字典成为学习的好帮手。如：查出字母的音节，查出单词的音标，查出名词的复数，查出动词的现在分词，查出动词的过去式，辨别可数名词和不可数名词，查出形容词的比较级和最高级，查出短语动词，认识字汇，等等。

3. 查字典比赛，时间为 10 分钟。同学们逐一查出试卷上各单词在字典里出现的页数，并注明页数、音标、中文意思、词性及相关例句等。试卷范例如下：

姓名________ 使用字典名称________

题号	单词	音标	中文意思	词性	页数	相关例句	本题得分	备注
1	happy							
2	humorous							
3	punctual							
4	determine							
5	towards							
6	vertical							
7	million							
8	thousand							
9	shell							
10	jasmine							
11	electronic							
12	address							
13	deed							
14	improve							
15	square							
16	background							
17	object							
18	subject							
19	yard							
20	porch							

注：试卷的题数和考点原则按学生年级的高低来具体安排。教师务必要提醒学生除了快速搜寻字义及音标外，也要注意抄录资料的正确性。

4. 在比赛结束也就是课堂的最后，教师可以提示学生使用字典的正确观念：

(1) 初学者可采用英汉字典找出字义，但是英英字典才是了解字义、语用的最佳工具书。初学者可以先用英汉字典查出字义，逐步参照英英、英汉双解字典，进而使用英英字典，找出完整的字义及用法。

(2) 若阅读的目的是为了了解文章的大意，则不需逐字查出生词的字义，仅需查出重要词汇的字义。若一一查询所有生词，则会接收零零散散的信息，反而妨碍阅读理解，使自己无法了解文章或段落的概要。

(3) 阅读时应善于利用上下文提供的线索来猜测字义，之后再查字典印证猜测的正确性。

(4) 字典除了用来搜寻字义，还提供了其他的重要资料。如不规则动词表、数词的读法、国名、英文名等。

【活动评述】

字典是学习英语不可或缺的工具，但我们只有懂得使用字典的技巧，才能让它成为自己的好帮手。教师配合教材设计查字典的作业，按部就班地培养学生查字典的好习惯，无形中能增进学生自主学习的能力。教师提供给学生的知识是有限的，但是经由字典的大门，学生就能进入丰富的语言世界。作为英语教师，我们应该引导学生打开字典、善用字典，让字典成为学生学习的好帮手！

【资料链接】

霍恩比、石孝殊等，《牛津高阶英汉双解词典》，商务印书馆，牛津大学出版社，2004

（深圳市南山中英文学校　高　洁）

二、读 写 篇

Reading

【设计理念】

根据小学生活泼好动，爱表现、爱竞争的心理特征，及他们对直观形象事物的认知特点，在“动态”的教学活动中，教师帮助学生掌握“静态”的课本知识，以培养其阅读能力。

【活动目标】

1. 语言的理解：文章字、词、句的理解。

2. 阅读技巧的培养：段落、篇章结构的分析。

3. 文化内涵的发掘：文化差异比较。

4. 语言运用：听、说、读、写的能力的培养。

5. 学习策略：小组学习和探究学习的策略。

【活动准备】

游戏、采访、画图等活动中需要涉及的素材。

【活动过程】

1. 借助直观教具的理解

(1) 简笔画。教师把备阅读的文章的内容以 3～4 幅简笔画的形式表现出来，图下面配以重点的词汇或句型。

(2) 电脑动画。教师利用电脑技术把备阅读的文章的内容做成有声、有色、有光、有影的动画片段，配上朗读录音，并在屏幕下方滚动播出文字。

(3) 录像。教师把文章内容预先摄制成录像，在课堂上播放。

(4) 戏剧表演。教师让几个英语基础好的同学，把备阅读的文章的内容表演出来，让其余的同学欣赏。

(5) 故事。教师以讲故事的方式，随时调节自己的语速、节奏、声调的高低、表情的变化等，引起学生的注意，帮助学生把握重难点、增强对所学材料的理解程度。

小结：直观形象的图片、声像，可以调动小学生多种感觉器官。教师通过动态的呈现方式，创设一些良好的学习情境，为学生理解抽象的知识提供丰富的感性材料，从而减少学生在学习中的困难，提高他们的学习兴趣和积极性，进而增强学生的思维能力。

2. 借助解决疑问的理解

(1) 听前设问。在学生进入课文之前，设计 1～2 个问题，让他们对内容有一个浅显、大概的了解。

(2) 边听边问。这一活动针对性比较强，阅读中的难点和重点可以在问题中解决。

(3) 听后发问。可以多提一些问题，让学生小组讨论。此类问题难度可加深一点，并可拓展到书本外。

小结：首先用设问的方法，吊学生的“胃口”，使他们渴望、追求新知奥秘。学生分析解决问题的过程就是培养思维能力的过程，在这一过程中，学生不仅获得了知识，更重要的是逐渐养成了良好的思维习惯，学会了思维的方法，最终形成质疑、提问的能力和习惯，达到能阅读的目的。教师也可以根据学生解决问题的情况，及时调整教学进度，改进教学方法、教学内容，优化课堂教学。

3. 借助小组合作活动的理解

(1) 小组讨论。分析文章的细节内容，可以采用小组探讨的形式。

(2) 故事拓展。小组中每个人以不同的人称来描述文章的内容。

(3) 表演。小组合作把文章内容表演出来，小组可以自己设计台词和对话。

(4) 采访。学生仿照文章内容，采访身边同学对某一观点的不同意见。

小结：在这类活动中，学生之间进行多向交流，不仅提高了他们学习的主动性和对学习的自我控制，而且也促进了他们心理品质的发展和社会技能的进步。

4. 借助游戏的理解

(1) 找朋友。教师把问答句分别写在小纸条上发给学生。学生相互读和听，找出与自己匹配的问答句。教师也可以把文章内容画成不同的几幅画，并把相应的描述图画的句子写在纸条上，让学生配对，看谁的画与谁的句子匹配。

(2) 填词配图。教师把文章的重点词或词组先挖去，然后让学生填写，并配以图画。

(3) Scramble。教师把文章的主要内容概括成 6～10 个句子，分别写在纸条上，打乱次序，让学生按正确的顺序排列。

(4) 编成儿歌或诗歌等。教师把文章的内容或里面出现的重点句型、词汇编在学生熟悉的儿歌中，学生读起来朗朗上口，易于他们更好地记忆和理解。

小结：游戏是儿童最喜爱的活动，他们做起游戏来，总是兴致勃勃，不知厌倦。游戏不仅能激发学生学习的兴趣，而且能检查学生对知识的掌握程度。

【教学案例】

A huge turnip

An old man and his wife lived on a farm. They had a dog and a cat. They worked in the field every day. They planted vegetables and sold them.

One day, the old man planted a turnip. The turnip grew and grew. It was a huge turnip. The old man wanted to pull out the turnip, but he could not pull it out. He called his wife: “Come and help me, dear.”

The old man and his wife pulled and pulled. They could not pull out the turnip. They called their dog: “Come and help us, Bobby.”

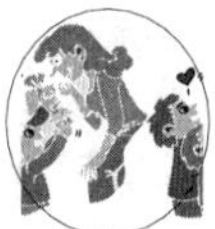

The old man, the old woman and the dog pulled and pulled. They could not pull out the turnip. They called the cat: "Come and help us, Kitty."

The old man, the old woman, the dog and the cat pulled and pulled: "One, two, three, pull!" Up came the huge turnip!

"What a huge turnip!" They exclaimed. They were very happy. They carried the huge turnip home.

1. 故事的呈现

(1) 教师在黑板上画一个很大的萝卜,问学生想不想听关于这个大萝卜的故事。

(2) 脑风暴游戏。教师问学生喜欢吃什么样的蔬菜,喜不喜欢吃大萝卜?

教师边画画边讲故事(一般 4～5 幅画),或让学生看动画。

在让学生看之前,教师先设计一两个比较简单的问题,如:

How many people and animals are there in the old man's home?

What did they carry home?

2. 故事的理解

(1) 教师多设计一点问题,让学生小组讨论,找出答案。例如:

Where did the old man and his wife live?

What did they sell?

The old man planted a turnip. Was it big or small?

Could the old man pull out the turnip?

Who helped him?

(2) 教师让学生同桌合作,采集信息填写事先准备的表格。学生根据文章内容,自己设计问题和答案,例如:

Where did the old man live?

	Questions	Answers
Who		
What		
Where		
How many		
Why		

(3) 判断正误的游戏。男女生比赛,看谁判断得又快又正确。例如:

(T) The old man lived on a farm.

(F) …

(4) 找朋友的游戏。教师在小纸条上写上问答句,让学生下座位,读给同学听,找与自己匹配的问句或答句(有的问句可以有几个答句)。例如:

Who lived with the old man? (答句有三个):

His wife.

A dog, Bobby.

A cat，Kitty.

（5）重点练习。文章在词汇和语法方面的重点是几个动词的过去式。教师设计练习如下面的五幅图，并分给五个小组。小组画完和填写完后，全班进行交流。（不一定每个同学把故事从头到尾地复述）

Fill in the blanks and finish the pictures：

Once upon a time，there was an old man and an old woman. They ______ on a farm. They ______ in the field every day. They ______ vegetables and ______ them.

They ________ a dog and a cat.

The old man ______ a turnip. It grew and it grew and it ______.

The old man，the old woman，the dog and the cat ______ out the turnip.

They ______ the turnip home.	

3. 故事的内涵挖掘

(1) 学生从故事中学到了什么？例如：

What do you learn from this story?

Do you like the cat and the dog? Why?

(2) 师：在实际生活中我们应该怎样呢？是不是也应该互相帮助呢？

例如：Interview some of your friends.

Name	What did he/she do to help others?

4. 故事的拓展

(1) 让学生续写故事。

(2) 让学生图文并茂地介绍种植萝卜的过程。

【资料链接】

1. 《牛津英语教师宝库》，华东师范大学出版社，牛津大学出版社，1998

2. 王电建、赖红玲，《小学英语教学法》，北京大学出版社，2002

3. How to teach English (Longman)

4. The storytelling handbook for primary teachers (Penguin books)

（深圳市南山外国语学校 葛岩峰）

In the Department Store

【设计理念】

在英语教学中，听、说、读、写是紧密相连的。教师在培养学生的听说能力的同时，也应注重培养其阅读的能力。阅读是学生吸收英语语言信息、增加语言知识、扩大词汇量的重要手段之一；而且阅读能力的提高能促进学生口语能力的发展。当然给小学生上阅读课，更要注重内容的趣味性，教师最好做到图文并茂，让学生易学易懂。

【教学目标】

1. 在多媒体网络环境下，利用网上丰富多彩、图文并茂的儿童英语小故事，加大学生英语的阅读量，提高其阅读兴趣和阅读理解能力。

2. 在阅读和理解短文的基础上，通过各种活动的操练，促使学生听、说、读、写的能力的提高。

3. 复习去商店购物的小对话，并运用“Can I help you?” “What do you want?” “Do you want…” “Which one do you want, the…one or the…one?”等句型进行对话。

【活动准备】

1. 教师事先根据“In the Department Store”改编的小短文。

2. 教师事先设计一些根据短文内容回答的问题。

3. 道具，如鲜花、文具、玩具、衣物、快餐食品等。

4. 多媒体设备。

5. 英语歌曲及英语小故事。

【活动过程】

1. Greetings and duty report

师生、生生之间用英语进行简短的问候，营造良好的课堂英语气氛，为下一步的学习做好铺垫。

2. Sentence game

挑出主要的句型让学生用学过的单词来造句。例如：

I want ________. I don't want any ________.

May I have ________?

Which ________ do you want, the ________ one or the ________?

学生运用句型造出的句子：

I want a red rose. I don't want the yellow rose. I want a long ruler. I don't want a short ruler. May I have a blue jacket, please?

Which toy plane do you want, the big one or the small one?

3. Read a passage

Tony, Jenny and Gogo are going shopping today. They are in a large department store. This is the ground floor. They can buy some stationery on this floor. Tony buys a pencil box and Jenny buys a green ruler. They spend 40 dollars. Gogo does not like stationery, he likes toys. So they come to the first floor. They can buy some toys on this floor. Gogo wants to buy a big teddy bear. Jenny wants to buy a yellow jacket. She can buy it on the second floor. What can they buy on the third floor? Furniture. There are some furniture on that floor.

学生看完短文后，小组合作，用开火车的方式进行短文的朗读。

4. Answer the questions

学生小组合作找答案。

问题如下：

(1) Where are Tony, Jenny and Gogo?

(2) What can they buy on the ground floor?

(3) Where can they buy toys?

(4) Which bear does Gogo want, the big one or the small one?

(5) How much are the pencil box and the ruler?

(6) Which jacket does Jenny want, the red one or the yellow one? What can they buy on the third floor?

5. Activities

教师设计模拟的商店，让学生用英语购物。

6. Extend readings

学生在教师的指导下阅读网上的英语小故事。

【活动评述】

虽然这堂课中的侧重点是阅读理解小短文，但学生在阅读理解小短文的基础上，还进行了许多听和说的练习活动，特别是在小组的模拟购物活动中。通过一系列的活动，学生的听与说都得到了很好的练习，他们的协作学习和自主学习的能力也得到了提高。最后的上网学习则拓展了学生的知识面，进一步激发了他们学习英语的兴趣。

【资料链接】

1. www. hellofox. com

2. Longman Intergrated Primary English

（深圳市南山区沙河小学　廖　玲）

Mickey's Birthday

【设计理念】

本课的活动设计旨在培养学生的阅读兴趣和综合运用语言的能力。设计遵循“以学生为本”的教育理念，通过复述故事的形式培养学生的语言表达能力，以自主排演的方式充分发挥学生的创新精神和表演天分。

【活动目标】

1. 通过自主阅读，让学生自己提出问题，培养其自学的能力。

2. 通过自主排演，激发学生的想像力和创造力，培养学生的创造性思维。

【活动准备】

1. 让每位学生自己设计一个头饰，准备参加 Mickey 的生日聚会。

2. 教师准备 Mickey 的头饰。

3. 教师在网上收集的图片。

4. 师生一起适当布置一下教室。

【活动过程】

学生头上戴着各种各样的头饰，有皇冠、月亮、太阳、蝴蝶、小猫、小狗……整个教室充满了庆祝生日的气氛。

1. 谈话导入，激发兴趣

T：Do you like Mickey?

Ss：Yes, we do.

T：Today is Mickey's birthday. His friends are having a party for him. Let's go to Mickey's party. OK?

Ss：OK!

T：But first, let's learn the lesson.

2. 自主阅读，巧设疑问

通过电脑整体呈现课文(两次)，让学生了解故事内容：

Today is Mickey's birthday. He's eight. Surprise! It's a party for Mickey. Mickey gets a very big present. Can you guess what it is? It's a piano. A big piano. What a surprise! Goofy is making a cake. It's a very big cake. His friends say: “Happy birthday, Mickey!” Mickey is very happy.

师：同学们，你们能找出文中的新单词吗？

生：能！

师：请大家用铅笔画出来，并猜猜它们的意思是什么？看谁最聪明。

（大家拿起铅笔迅速地画起来）

师：好！同学们都做得很好。让我们一起来学习这些单词吧。

（通过电脑呈现单词图片，让学生跟读）

生：我们会读了。

师：你们能根据文章的内容提一些问题吗？如果提得好，有红花奖励。

S1：How old is Mickey?

S2：Whose birthday is today?

S3：Is Mickey happy?

S4：What's Mickey's present?

S5：Who is making a cake?

S6：Does he have a birthday cake?

S7：What do his friends say?

师：大家提得非常好。（给提问好的同学发红花）接下来，我们来玩一个男女同学的夺红旗比赛，好不好？

生：（兴奋地说）好！

3. 自主创新，复述故事

通过以上的学习过程，学生对课文已经有了一定的理解，教师可以在此基础上引导学生复述故事的内容。

师：同学们都认真学了课文，也对 Mickey 的生日聚会很感兴趣。现在我们来讲讲这个故事，相信你们一定会讲得很好！你们先在小组里试着讲一讲。

（学生在小组里复述故事，并试着将自己的语言整合到课文中。教师深入各小组有针对性地进行指导……）

师：现在请各小组的代表来复述这个故事。

S1 站起来，镇定自若地复述道：

Today is Saturday. It's Mickey's birthday. He is eight years old. There's a party for Mickey. He gets many presents and a big birthday cake. His friends say happy birthday to him! and sing happy birthday song to him. Mickey is smiling. He's very happy.

师：Wonderful!

4. 自主排演，深化理解

在学生对课文的内容有了较深理解的基础上，让他们充分发挥自己的想像力和创造力，把故事表演出来。教师最后给表演得好的小组发最佳表演奖。

【活动评述】

教学中，教师创设情景，给学生提供充分的表现自我的机会。学生们自己探索、自主排演，积极参与，学习兴趣浓厚，整个课堂教学过程轻松而愉快……

【资料链接】

http：//www.disney.com

（深圳市南山区南山小学　罗　红）

Chinese New Year

【设计理念】

“说写转换”关注的是学生学习的过程和学习的方法，并满足不同学习水平的学生的学习需要。本设计通过进行充分的“说”，然后转换为“写”，即“说中学，说后写”，激发学生的学习积极性，使“说”英语成为一种习惯。我们认为，只有学生会说，说好了，培养学生写的能力才能落到实处。

【活动目标】

1. 复习和巩固已学过的词和句型。

2. 让学生进行充分的“说”，最后实现“写”。

【活动准备】

1. 每个同学想出自己过年准备做的五件事。

2. 多媒体教学课件、词卡、图片等。

【活动过程】

1. 自由会话活动

教师让学生围绕以下问题展开会话活动：

When is Chinese New Year?

What do you do at Chinese New Year?

What makes you happy at Chinese New Year?

Do you have lots of fun?

Are you going to visit friends / get lucky money / buy new clothes / clean the house ?

2. 听说结合活动

(1) 学生听、读课文，知道过年时都干些什么。

(2) 学生两人一组，进行角色朗读表演。

3. 说的活动

(1) 展示一组多媒体画面(如孩子穿新衣，得到红包，走亲访友，打扫卫生，吃饭等等)，让学生根据画面进行发散性思维，从不同的角度叙述每幅画的内容。

(2) 学生四人一小组进行讨论，每组谈论 2～3 幅图画的内容。

(3) 学生以小组的方式进行说话比赛，教师板书关键词组。

(4) 教师请学生任选三幅画，先与同桌编一段故事，然后参与说故事的比赛。

4. 写的活动

(1) 教师将上一环节的关键词写在黑板上，如：get lucky money，buy new clothes，Happy New Year，clean the house，visit family and friends，eat a big dinner 等。

(2) 学生根据上一环节的说图活动，利用词语写出不同形式的短文，如记叙文、对话、书信或贺卡等。

5. 展示活动

由于学生都有过年的亲身感受，又经过以上的练习，他们写起短文来就非常顺利，有介绍过年风俗习惯的，有写自己过年感受和新年打算的，也有给朋友写信和贺卡祝贺新年的，形式多样，内容丰富。Kate 在作文中写到：At Chinese New Year, we eat big dinners, wear new clothes and put on decorations. Marry 则写到：Chinese New Year is coming soon. I am very happy. I have lots of fun…

【活动评述】

"说写转换"让学生在"说"中学习英语，在"说"中获得知识，在"说"中培养能力，最后自然地落实到"写"上。这个设计，从学生的兴趣、生活经验和认知水平出发，通过他们自身的体验、实践、参与、合作与交流的学习方式，发展了学生综合语言运用的能力，使语言学习过程成为培养学生形成积极的情感态度和自主学习能力的过程。

【资料链接】

1. Chinese New Year, Book 7, *Primary English For China*

2. 陈少敏，《小学教学全书——英语卷》

(深圳市南山区南头城小学　付晓霞)

My Favorite Festival

【设计理念】

“人的活动是社会及其全部价值存在与发展的本源，是人的生命以及作为个性的发展与形成的源泉。教育学离开了活动问题就不可能解决任何一项教育、教学、发展的任务。”英语科的教学是以进行中西方不同语言文化背景下相互间交流为目的的师生双边活动，其课堂教学目标应该在交往与活动中达成。

【活动目标】

通过本课的活动，使学生对中西方重要节日、风俗有初步的了解，并能较流利地运用英语就相关内容进行口头交流。教师通过大量的口语练习，培养学生的笔头书写能力。

【活动准备】

1. 将课堂布置成马蹄形小组的形式，以利于小组与小组及组内成员间的交往与活动。

2. 课件准备：中国人过春节的喜庆片段，端午节、万圣节、圣诞节、复活节等中西方重要节日及风俗的相关场景等。

3. 教师准备猜谜用的小纸条。

4. 教师提供每位同学书写短文所用的纸张。

【活动过程】

1. 营造课堂氛围。

课堂教学氛围的营造对教学效果的达成起不容忽视的作用！我走进教室，神情严肃地宣布：“We are going to have a test at this class!”(这节课考试!)想像一下学生们的反应！大家面面相觑！“Great!”我心里暗暗说道。就在大家开始无奈地收拾桌上的东西时，我又笑道：“Happy April Fool’s Day!”(愚人节快乐!)，并引导学生回答：“Happy April Fool’s Day!”可以想像，同学们对愚人节一定印象深刻。

2. 组织“热身”交流。

“April Fool’s Day is a festival. We play tricks at this festival. Do you like this festival?”教师强调生词“festival”的拼读。教师采访几位同学：“Do you like April Fool’s Day? What do we do at it?”，再安排同学在组内相互问答……

3. 拓展“交流”范围。

教师打开课件，播放一段中国人过大年的喜庆场面，用生动的画面和立体的音效吸引学生的眼球和耳朵！然后问道："Is it April Fool's Day? What festival is it? Do you like it?"基于以前的知识，学生们都能应对。教师循序渐进，引导大家思考："I like Chinese New Year. I don't go to school at Chinese New Year. I can go back to my hometown to visit my family. What do you do at Chinese New Year?"鼓励学生进行交流。

4. 加强合作，自主学习新知识。

"What are these festivals? And what do people do at these festivals? Do you like them?"教师继续播放其他节日风俗的片段，同时强调生词的认读和拼写，鼓励学生做好笔记。教师大胆放手，让学生在小组内自己认读生词，自主开展问答。

5. 开展"问答"比赛，巩固口头表达。

教师利用肢体语言，比划穿上新衣给大家拜年的动作，提问："What festival is this? What do you do at this festival?"引导同学们对答："It's Chinese New Year! We visit friends at this festival."教师抓住机会，再次提出问题："I like Chinese New Year because I can go back to my hometown to visit my family. Why do you like it?"强调生词 why 和 because 的拼读，带读几遍后，挑一位同学回答问题。答对问题的同学可以得分，还可以任意提问其他组成员。如此循环，许多同学就有了 show 一把的成功感……多些品尝胜利滋味的机会能令学生始终保持饱满的学习热情。

6. 组织游戏，强化认读和口头表达。

教师故作神秘地把写好节日名称的纸条散发给每个小组，请大家准备两分钟后，用自己的语言描述条儿上的节日，以便其他小组猜测纸条上的内容。教师要求小组内所有成员必须发言，且内容不能雷同。教师给出评定标准：语言准确流畅，令猜谜者一击即中，双方得分；若因为语言不够准确，令其他组猜不出正确答案的，则要倒扣分！

【活动评述】

教师是课堂上的灵魂人物，他可以"满堂灌"，让讲台变成他自己的舞台，使学生成为他一个人的观众；他也可以活跃于同学当中，穿针引线，调动孩子们的交往动机，让他们经验共享、学会合作、发现自我。

【资料链接】

1. 休金娜，《活动——教育过程的基础》，人民教育出版社，1991

2. 高峡等，《活动课程的理论与实践》，上海科技教育出版社，1997

（深圳市南山区大勘小学　黄　瑛）

Helping at Home (3)

【设计理念】

情景教学,可以创造一个积极、生动、活泼的课堂气氛。运用情景教学进行语言训练,将大大提高教学的效果。合作学习,可以让学生自觉、自愿、自由地投入到学习活动中去,成为学习的主人。

【活动目标】

通过小组学习,增加学生参与操练的机会,让同学之间互助互学,提高班级整体的写作水平。

【活动准备】

教师将学生分为五个活动小组,并准备扫把、碗碟,浇花用品等工具。

【活动过程】

1. 创设情景,进行语言片段的训练。

(1) Do you help at home?

(2) What housework do you do at home?

(3) How often do you do it?

(4) When do you do it?

教师请在家勤做家务的同学表演做家务,要求大家注意观察和记录。然后以小组为单位,以表演者为主人翁,让学生写作 Helping at home 的短文。

为了启发学生,教师指着上台表演的 S1 问大家:

Who is he? Is he a boy? How old is he? Is he your friend(classmate,neighbour)?

这样一来,同学们很快就写开了:

××× is a boy. He's a student. He's…

文章的开头组织好后,教师、S1 以及全班同学进行这样的对话:

T: Do you always help at home, S1?

S1: Yes, I always help at home.

T: How often do you help at home?

S1: I always help at home.

T: How often does he help at home?

Ss: He always helps at home.

T: What housework do you do at home? Please do a show for us.

（S1 做动作）

T：What are you doing?

S1：I'm sweeping the floor.

T：When do you sweep the floor?

S1：I usually sweep the floor in the morning.

T：When does he sweep the floor?

Ss：He usually sweeps the floor in the morning.

S1 继续表演 Set the table，wash the dishes，clean a room，make the bed…

在这个过程中，学生一边看表演，一边回答老师的问题，并把有关的句子写下来。在指导学生进行作文的结尾时，教师又向同学提出了这样的问题：

（1）S1 always helps at home. Is he a good boy?

（2）Should we learn from him?

（3）Should we help others?

2. 小组协作，生生互动。

这一阶段的活动内容是要求学生把刚才记下的有关 S1 做家务的资料，通过小组的合作，整理成一篇文章，并打印在电脑上。小组活动的时间为 10 分钟。作文示范：

Helping at Home

S1 is a boy. He's a student. He's eleven. He's our classmate. He's our friend, too.

S1 always helps at home. He usually sweeps the floor in the morning. He makes his bed every day. He sometimes sets the bed. He's a good boy. He…

We should learn from him. We should help others, too.

【活动评述】

用英语写作是小学教学的一大难题。但是根据儿童学习语言的规律，以表演创设情景，用情景教学来激发学生表达的欲望、启发学生的思维、给学生提供作文的素材，会大大提高教学的效果。用小组协作的教学活动让学生完成作文，落实了学生自主学习、合作学习、探究学习的任务型教学，使学生真正成为课堂的主人翁。

【资料链接】

1. 章兼中，《小学英语教学》，山西高校联合出版社，1996

2. 李吉林，《情景教学——情景教育》，山东教育出版社，2002

（深圳市南山区南头城小学　李育香）

Onset—Rhyme—Writing

【设计理念】

语音是语言教学的重要内容之一。语音学习是一个习惯形成的过程，而语音习惯的形成需要多听、多练、多模仿。因此，相对而言，语音教学是比较单调和枯燥的。韵律诗大多短小明快、节奏感强，且富于韵味，在语音教学中常使用韵律诗进行巩固操练是非常重要的。

“写”是语言的综合运用，是表现创新思维的手段。因此，在学生已大量模仿和感知了语音和韵律的基础上，我们大胆地进行韵律诗写作的教学尝试，设计以学生为主体的教学活动，采用任务型的课堂教学模式，结合“兴趣、情景、活动”教学法，以求达到学习、巩固语音，运用知识，培养学生主动学习、团结合作、大胆实践、勇于创新的目的。

【活动目标】

1. 学生学习下列音素、单词和小诗，能用正确的语调进行朗读，并能正确理解诗的内容。

ou out around shout playground

Let's go out
And run around.
We can shout
In the playground.

2. 学生能运用所学的语音知识拼读新单词。

3. 学生能用所学单词进行简单的韵律诗写作。

4. 学生能与小组内其他成员团结协作共同完成任务。

【活动准备】

1. 配套电脑光盘，投影仪，音标卡，韵律诗(含相关音素)，各色磁铁(供小组竞赛时分组用)。

2. 学生按小组就座。

【活动过程】

Step 1：Warm-up

rhyme：I'm a Little Teapot

I'm a little teapot,
Short and stout.

Here's my handle,
Here's my spout.
When the water's boiling,
Hear me shout.
Tip me over,
Pour me out.

(歌谣热身)借助投影仪,学生看着优美的图文和教师一起边说边模仿茶壶的形状。

Step 2：Lead In

1. 让学生再读歌谣,找出 stout, spout, shout, out 四个词发音的共同点。(它们都含有字母 ou 组合,而且都发[au])

教师巧妙利用歌谣进行启发,引导学生发现学习的重点,并初步感知韵律诗的格式特点,体现出以学生为主体的教学思想。

2. 教师讲解示范[au]的发音口型,要求学生模仿,并进行检查。

Step 3：Listen and Speak

1. 教师用投影仪呈现例词,鼓励学生运用已有的知识去尝试拼读单词。

T：Can we run around the classroom? Can we run around the playground? We can shout in the playground. We can't shout in the classroom.

2. 学生仔细听录音然后跟读。

3. 学生分组竞赛读。教师要求学生分别用升调和降调读音素和例词,为下一步学习韵律诗做好语调上的准备。

4. 教师鼓励学生尝试读韵律诗,并对他们的大胆尝试予以肯定。“You can read quite well. Now let's listen and check, ok?”学生仔细听然后跟读,并注意自己语调的升降和节奏感。

5. 把诗分为三拍,学生分组竞赛打拍读,节奏和语调最好的小组为胜利组。

6. 学生找出押韵的词和音素,进一步明确韵律诗的特点。

Step 4：Exercise

1. 教师用投影仪呈现一些句子,每句均有一个以上含有字母 ou 的新单词。学生在小组内合作尝试拼读单词,然后大声朗读出来。

2. 教师让学生找出已学过的含有字母 ou 的单词。

Step 5：Ryhme Work

通过前面的学习,学生已积累一定数量的词汇,对韵律诗的特点也有了较清晰的认识,思维得到了启发。这时,教师鼓励学生以小组为单位,用含有字母 ou 的单词写一首韵律诗。学生习作示范：

1. Whose house?
   Whose house?
   It's mouse's.
2. I'm a little mouse.
   I have a small mouth.
   Let's play in my house.

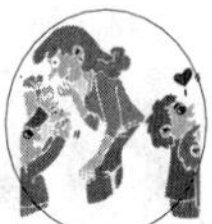

3. Look at the mouse.
It's in the teapot.
Look at the teapot.
It's in the trousers.
Look at the trousers.
They're in the house.

4. There's a mouse.
Wearing trousers.
On the cloud.

5. I'm trousers.
Long and stout.
You're wearing me.
You're very pretty.

Step 6：Extended Activities

让学生根据自己的爱好和特长，选择几种作业形式：

1. 有节奏、有感情地朗读韵律诗。
2. 给自己作的诗配图。
3. 自行设计作业，如表演诗歌、抄写等。（充分尊重学生意愿）

【活动评述】

学习英语，不仅要通过耳听、口说、眼看，还要通过手写。从心理学的角度分析，写属于运动觉。运动觉比听觉、视觉等留在大脑中的印象更深，更容易被理解和掌握。在语音教学中，通过听、说、读等手段大量输入音素、语调和韵律的信息后，以写的形式输出的语音知识和技能就能更牢固地被学生掌握。虽然学生写的韵律诗还相当稚嫩，但我们完全有理由相信，那神奇的语感的种子已在学生的心田里扎了根。

【资料链接】

1.《英语课程标准（实验稿）》，北京师范大学出版社，2001
2. 章兼中，《小学英语教育学》，山西高校联合出版社，1996
3. http：//www. xinzhitang. com. cn

（深圳市南山区大勘小学　梁清颖）

Class Library Rules

【设计理念】

设计遵循任务型教学的基本原则，从意义到知识开展教学活动，在大班教学的现实中设计合理、有效的教学活动，激发学生学习英语的兴趣。本设计在提高学生会话能力的基础上提高写的能力；在发展学生知识和技能的同时，培养学生的情感、态度和价值观；并加强学生语言的实践，培养其创新意识。

【活动目标】

1. 让学生复习巩固所学的用语和句型，加强语言实践。

2. 通过学生的写作实践，培养学生的思维能力、想像力和写作能力。

3. 通过小组合作学习，培养学生的团队合作精神。

4. 培养学生的公共道德意识。

【活动准备】

水彩笔或蜡笔若干、钢笔、透明胶、剪刀、A3 白纸十多张、实物投影等。

【活动过程】

1. 设置情景，激发兴趣

师：我们班将在教室后面开办一个小小的图书角，利用班费购买一部分图书，每个同学再从家中带几本书。大家想想，如何将我班的图书角办好？我们应该注意哪些事项？我们应该做些什么，不应该做什么？

Ss：We should/shouldn't…

2. 黑板板书，给出样板

根据学生的回答，老师请部分学生上台，设计并画出图书角要张贴的标志，请台下的同学来猜，最后师生一起写出英文句子以说明标志的意思。

3. 小组合作，积极准备

四人小组合作，在老师发的统一规格的白纸上，用水彩笔或钢笔，在老师规定的十分钟内完成班级图书角制度(Class Library Rules)的写作任务。教师提醒学生想一想：What should we do? What shouldn't we do? 写作要求图文并茂，既要画标志又要写句子。最后小组之间比一比：看哪一组的学生在规定时间内写得最多、最准确，同时书写规范、设计精美。

4. 上台汇报，一展风采

各小组派代表上台宣读所写的内容，宣读的同时将纸张放在实物投影下，让班上每个学生都看得到。师生一起边看边读,边看边听。师生一起统计每组的句数,评比出哪组句子最多、哪组书法最工整、哪组排版设计最优秀、哪组准确率最高、哪组最合作等。

学生习作示范:

Class Library Rules

(1) Don't tear the pages.

(2) Don't draw in the books.

(3) Don't write in the books.

(4) No eating.

(5) Keep quiet.

(6) Return the books on time.

(7) Keep the books clean.

(8) Don't run in the class library.

…

5. 张贴作品,享受成功

每一组将自己的作品张贴在教室的墙上。老师在学生完成后小结:希望同学们在使用班级或学校的图书角的时候,遵守自己订下的规则。

6. 独立作业,巩固所学

教师要求每个学生回去后做一张有关 Class Library Rules 的海报,可手工,也可电脑制作,要求有标志、有文字。

【活动评述】

在任务型教学活动的设计中,通过设置情景来操作活动,往往可以事半功倍。同时,任务的设计还要考虑到其他的教学原则,如培养学生问题解决的能力。老师在设计中注重培养学生文化知识的同时,还加强了对学生思想感情、道德品质等方面的教育及合作精神的培养,这个设计体现了以人为本、以学生为中心、以情为重的教学思想,而且简单易行,可操作性强。

【资料链接】

New Integrated Primary English

(深圳市南山区外国语学校　杨　毅)

Writing

【设计理念】

《英语课程标准》总目标是在语言技能、语言知识、情感态度、学习策略和文化意识发展的基础上培养学生的综合语言运用能力。而我们在教学中强化写的训练能够提高学生书面表达的能力，从而促使学生多方面的发展。本篇教学活动设计所努力追求的便是这样一种教学理念。

【活动目标】

1. 通过写的活动，让学生能使用“There will be…”“…will do something.”等句型来描述未来场所的情景，从而提高书面表达的能力。

2. 通过趣味性、激励性和创造性的活动激发学生学习英语的兴趣，培养其良好的学习习惯，并拓展他们的视野，发挥他们的想像力，培养他们热爱生活的高尚情操。

【活动准备】

学生自己收集相关知识的词汇、剪贴或画出有关“未来的××(场所)”的图画，为写小作文做好准备。

【活动过程】

1. 猜猜写写，激趣热身

老师用猜谜语的形式听写已学的单词，激发学生的学习热情。

T：Now take out your exercise books，please. I'm going to say some riddles. You will guess and write down these words.

例如：

> Usually there is a TV and a long sofa in it. We can watch TV on the sofa. What is it? (It's a living room)

这是一项热身运动。传统的单纯的听写活动本身是比较枯燥的，但一旦引入了“猜”的活动就会增强其趣味性，使学生较快地集中注意力，迅速进入教学活动中。

2. 连线写句，多多益善

在投影上给出一些连线材料，让学生仿照所给的句型进行连线写句，教师在座位间巡视指导。(规定时间内看谁写得多，写得有趣，然后让胜出的同学说说这些句子)

T：Make sentences with the following phrases，using“There will be…”and“…will do something”.

（1）看谁写得多

a telephone	a living room
a computer	a bedroom
a wardrobe	a garden
a fridge	a kitchen
a swimming pool	a library
a sofa	a bathroom

There will be a telephone in a bathroom.

（2）看谁写得有趣

headteacher	clean the lamp	kitchen
headmaster	set the table	bedroom
art teacher	water the plant	living room
music teacher	watch TV	bathroom
English teacher	listen to music	library
Chinese teacher	sweep the stairs	garden

My English teacher will watch TV in the kitchen.

“写”这种综合性活动的难度相对较大，特别是对于小学生而言。因此教师要设计循序渐进的“阶梯”，设置一定的梯度，允许学生从比较基础的能力层级开始一步一步地提高。在“攀登”的过程中教师要努力增强途中的趣味性，使学生的疲劳度弱化。连线活动是在已学内容的基础上进行的，较易激活学生原有的认知结构，基本上是一种复现活动，难度较小，且有一定的趣味性。这种在有意义的情景中的连词成句的活动，可以帮助学生强化对词语的记忆，加深对词语的理解。另外，已学的相关语言知识在大脑中的多次复现，又可以帮助学生构建新的知识框架，培养其运用语言的习惯和能力。

3．画图作文，各显其能

学生拿出自己事先设计好的图画“未来的××（场所）”，然后以小组为单位分工合作，根据大家所设计的图画中最优秀的作品写出一篇短文（未来的家、未来的学校、未来的教室……），并在班上展示。最后师生一起评出“最佳设计师”（共设三个奖项：最佳绘画、最佳作文、综合最佳），既让不同学生的才华得到充分的展示，又培养学生集体合作的精神。

学生作文示范：

The House of the Future

This is my house of the future.

In the living room, there will be a big TV and a long sofa. I will watch TV and play there.

In the bedrooms, there will be big beds and wardrobes. I will sleep and hang up my clothes.

In the library, there will be a lot of books and CDs. I will read books and listen to music there.

The kitchen will be big. I will cook and eat there.

The School of the Future

This is our school of the future.

In the classrooms, there will be long tables and long chairs. Everyone has a computer. We will study and play computer games there.

In the corridors, there will be a lot of plants and flowers. They are beautiful. We will walk and play in the corridors.

In the playground, there will be a swimming pool. It is big. We will swim in summer.

图画这种儿童喜用乐为的形式的介入，增添了语言学习过程中的乐趣，还起到了强化巩固学习效果的作用。

4. 书面评价，课外延伸

全体学生在课后以书面的形式在大家的展示作品中评选出“我最喜爱的作品”，并写出自己的理由。例如：

S1：I choose “The House of the Future” because there will be a CD player in the library. He/She will listen to music there. That will be happy.

S2：I choose “The School of the Future” because there will be a swimming pool in the playground. Everyone will swim after school in summer. It will be fun.

这里采用的是综合评价中的同伴互评的模式，这种模式一方面改变了教师评价时“居高临下”的压力，另一方面通过书面评价的过程，给学生一次很好的书面表达训练。

【活动评述】

这个设计贴近学生实际，采取“问题情境＋解决方法”的模式，循序渐进地落实到写，使学生的知识建构具有现实的意义，从而使其书面表达能力得到了较好的发展。设计让学生成为课堂活动的主体，将教授内容与生活空间、学生情感与外部世界、学生已有的知识积累与学习的可能空间有效地结合起来，并创设情趣共生的教学情境，使学生能在发展思维活力中体验探索发现的乐趣。

【资料链接】

1. 禹明，《探索新型的英语教学》，四川文艺出版社，2001

2. 禹明，《小学英语教学理念与教学示例》，华南理工大学出版社，2003

（深圳市南山区月亮湾小学　李　军）

北京大学出版社

教育出版中心 精品图书

21世纪特殊教育创新教材·理论与基础系列

特殊教育的哲学基础 方俊明 主编 36元
特殊教育的医学基础 张 婷 主编 36元
特殊教育导论（第二版） 雷江华 主编 45元
特殊教育学（第二版） 雷江华 方俊明 主编 43元
特殊儿童心理学（第二版） 方俊明 雷江华 主编 39元
特殊教育史 朱宗顺 主编 39元
特殊教育研究方法（第二版） 杜晓新 宋永宁等 主编 39元
特殊教育发展模式 任颂羔 主编 33元
特殊儿童心理与教育（第二版） 杨广学 张巧明 王 芳 主编 36元
教育康复学导论 杜晓新 黄昭鸣 55元
特殊儿童病理学 王和平 杨长江 48元

21世纪特殊教育创新教材·发展与教育系列

视觉障碍儿童的发展与教育 邓 猛 编著 33元
听觉障碍儿童的发展与教育 贺荟中 编著 38元
智力障碍儿童的发展与教育 刘春玲 马红英 编著 32元
学习困难儿童的发展与教育 赵 微 编著 39元
自闭症谱系障碍儿童的发展与教育 周念丽 编著 32元
情绪与行为障碍儿童的发展与教育 李闻戈 编著 36元
超常儿童的发展与教育（第二版） 苏雪云 张 旭 编著 39元

21世纪特殊教育创新教材·康复与训练系列

特殊儿童应用行为分析 李 芳 李 丹 编著 36元
特殊儿童的游戏治疗 周念丽 编著 30元
特殊儿童的美术治疗 孙 霞 编著 38元
特殊儿童的音乐治疗 胡世红 编著 32元
特殊儿童的心理治疗（第二版） 杨广学 编著 45元
特殊教育的辅具与康复 蒋建荣 编著 29元
特殊儿童的感觉统合训练 王和平 编著 45元
孤独症儿童课程与教学设计 王 梅 著 37元

自闭谱系障碍儿童早期干预丛书

如何发展自闭谱系障碍儿童的沟通能力 朱晓晨 苏雪云 29元
如何理解自闭谱系障碍和早期干预 苏雪云 32元
如何发展自闭谱系障碍儿童的社会交往能力 吕 梦 杨广学 33元
如何发展自闭谱系障碍儿童的自我照料能力 倪萍萍 周 波 32元
如何在游戏中干预自闭谱系障碍儿童 朱 瑞 周念丽 32元
如何发展自闭谱系障碍儿童的感知和运动能力 韩文娟，徐芳，王和平 32元
如何发展自闭谱系障碍儿童的认知能力 潘前前 杨福义 39元
自闭症谱系障碍儿童的发展与教育 周念丽 32元
如何通过音乐干预自闭谱系障碍儿童 张正琴 36元
如何通过画画干预自闭谱系障碍儿童 张正琴 36元
如何运用ACC促进自闭谱系障碍儿童的发展 苏雪云 36元
孤独症儿童的关键性技能训练法 李 丹 45元
自闭症儿童家长辅导手册 雷江华 35元
孤独症儿童课程与教学设计 王 梅 37元
融合教育理论反思与本土化探索 邓 猛 58元
自闭症谱系障碍儿童家庭支持系统 孙玉梅 36元

特殊学校教育·康复·职业训练丛书（黄建行 雷江华 主编）

信息技术在特殊教育中的应用 55元
智障学生职业教育模式 36元
特殊教育学校学生康复与训练 59元
特殊教育学校校本课程开发 45元
特殊教育学校特奥运动项目建设 49元

21世纪学前教育规划教材

学前教育概论 李生兰 主编 49元
学前教育管理学 王 雯 45元
幼儿园歌曲钢琴伴奏教程 果旭伟 39元
幼儿园舞蹈教学活动设计与指导 董 丽 36元
实用乐理与视唱 代 苗 40元
学前儿童美术教育 冯婉贞 45元
学前儿童科学教育 洪秀敏 39元
学前儿童游戏 范明丽 39元
学前教育研究方法 郑福明 39元
外国学前教育史 郭法奇 39元
学前教育政策与法规 魏 真 36元
学前心理学 涂艳国、蔡 艳 36元
学前教育理论与实践教程 王 维 王维娅 孙 岩 39元
学前儿童数学教育 赵振国 39元

大学之道丛书

市场化的底限　[美] 大卫·科伯 著 59元
大学的理念　[英] 亨利·纽曼 著 49元
哈佛：谁说了算　[美] 理查德·布瑞德利 著 48元
麻省理工学院如何追求卓越
[美] 查尔斯·维斯特 著 35元
大学与市场的悖论　[美] 罗杰·盖格 著 48元
高等教育公司：营利性大学的崛起
[美] 理查德·鲁克 著 38元
公司文化中的大学：大学如何应对市场化压力
[美] 埃里克·古尔德 著 40元
美国高等教育质量认证与评估
[美] 美国中部州高等教育委员会 编 36元
现代大学及其图新
[美] 谢尔顿·罗斯布莱特 著 60元
美国文理学院的兴衰——凯尼恩学院纪实
[美] P. F.克鲁格 著 42元
教育的终结：大学何以放弃了对人生意义的追求
[美] 安东尼·T.克龙曼 著 35元
大学的逻辑（第三版）　张维迎 著 38元
我的科大十年（续集）　孔宪铎 著 35元
高等教育理念　[英] 罗纳德·巴尼特 著 45元
美国现代大学的崛起　[美] 劳伦斯·维赛 著 66元
美国大学时代的学术自由
[美] 沃特·梅兹格 著 39元
美国高等教育通史　[美] 亚瑟·科恩 著 59元
美国高等教育史　[美] 约翰·塞林 著 69元
哈佛通识教育红皮书　哈佛委员会撰 38元
高等教育何以为"高"——牛津导师制教学反思
[英] 大卫·帕尔菲曼 著 39元
印度理工学院的精英们
[印度] 桑迪潘·德布 著 39元
知识社会中的大学　[英] 杰勒德·德兰迪 著 32元
高等教育的未来：浮言、现实与市场风险
[美] 弗兰克·纽曼等 著 39元
后现代大学来临？ [英] 安东尼·史密斯等 主编 32元
美国大学之魂　[美] 乔治·M.马斯登 著 58元
大学理念重审：与纽曼对话
[美] 雅罗斯拉夫·帕利坎 著 40元
学术部落及其领地——当代学术界生态揭秘（第二版）　[英] 托尼·比彻 保罗·特罗勒尔 著 33元
德国古典大学观及其对中国大学的影响（第二版）
陈洪捷 著 42元
转变中的大学：传统、议题与前景　郭为藩 著 23元
学术资本主义：政治、政策和创业型大学
[美] 希拉·斯劳特 拉里·莱斯利 著 36元
21世纪的大学　[美] 詹姆斯·杜德斯达 著 38元
美国公立大学的未来
[美] 詹姆斯·杜德斯达 弗瑞斯·沃马克 著 30元
东西象牙塔　孔宪铎 著 32元
理性捍卫大学　眭依凡 著 49元

学术规范与研究方法系列

社会科学研究方法100问　[美] 萨子金德 著 38元
如何利用互联网做研究　[爱尔兰] 杜恰泰 著 38元
如何为学术刊物撰稿：写作技能与规范（英文影印版）　[英] 罗薇娜·莫 编著 26元
如何撰写和发表科技论文（英文影印版）
[美] 罗伯特·戴 等著 39元
如何撰写与发表社会科学论文：国际刊物指南
蔡今忠 著 35元
如何查找文献　[英] 萨莉拉·姆齐 著 35元
给研究生的学术建议　[英] 戈登·鲁格 等著 26元
科技论文写作快速入门
[瑞典] 比约·古斯塔维 著 19元
社会科学研究的基本规则（第四版）
[英] 朱迪斯·贝尔 著 32元
做好社会研究的10个关键
[英] 马丁·丹斯考姆 著 20元
如何写好科研项目申请书
[美] 安德鲁·弗里德兰德 等著 28元
教育研究方法（第六版）
[美] 乔伊斯·高尔 等著 88元
高等教育研究：进展与方法
[英] 马尔科姆·泰特 著 25元
如何成为学术论文写作高手　华莱士 著 49元
参加国际学术会议必须要做的那些事
华莱士 著 32元
如何成为优秀的研究生　布卢姆 著 38元

21世纪高校职业发展读本

如何成为卓越的大学教师　肯·贝恩 著 32元
给大学新教员的建议　罗伯特·博伊斯 著 35元
如何提高学生学习质量
[英] 迈克尔·普洛瑟 等著 35元
学术界的生存智慧　[美] 约翰·达利 等主编 35元
给研究生导师的建议（第2版）
[英] 萨拉·德拉蒙特 等著 30元

21世纪教师教育系列教材·物理教育系列

中学物理微格教学教程（第二版）
张军朋 詹伟琴 王 恬 编著 32元

中学物理科学探究学习评价与案例
张军朋 许桂清 编著 32元

物理教学论 邢红军 著 49元

中学物理教学评价与案例分析
王建中 孟红娟 著 38元

21世纪教育科学系列教材·学科学习心理学系列

数学学习心理学（第二版）
孔凡哲 曾 峥 编著 38元

语文学习心理学 董蓓菲 编著 39元

21世纪教师教育系列教材

教育学基础 庞守兴 主编 40元
教育学 余文森 王 晞 主编 26元
教育研究方法 刘淑杰 主编 45元
教育心理学 王晓明 主编 55元
心理学导论 杨凤云 主编 46元
教育心理学概论 连 榕 罗丽芳 主编 42元
课程与教学论 李 允 主编 42元
教师专业发展导论 于胜刚 主编 42元
学校教育概论 李清雁 主编 42元
现代教育评价教程（第二版） 吴 钢 主编 45元
教师礼仪实务 刘 霄 主编 36元
家庭教育新论 闫旭蕾 杨 萍 主编 39元
中学班级管理 张宝书 主编 39元
教育职业道德 刘亭亭 39元
教师心理健康 张怀春 39元
现代教育技术 冯玲玉 39元
青少年发展与教育心理学 张 清 42元
课程与教学论 李 允 42元
课堂教学艺术（第二版） 孙菊如 陈春荣 49元

21世纪教师教育系列教材·初等教育系列

小学教育学 田友谊 主编 39元
小学教育学基础 张永明 曾 碧 主编 42元
小学班级管理 张永明 宋彩琴 主编 39元
初等教育课程与教学论 罗祖兵 主编 45元
小学教育研究方法 王红艳 主编 39元

教师资格认定及师范类毕业生上岗考试辅导教材

教育学 余文森 王 晞 主编 26元
教育心理学概论 连 榕 罗丽芳 主编 42元

21世纪教师教育系列教材·学科教育心理学系列

语文教育心理学 董蓓菲 编著 39元
生物教育心理学 胡继飞 编著 45元

21世纪教师教育系列教材·学科教学论系列

新理念化学教学论（第二版） 王后雄 主编 45元

新理念科学教学论（第二版）
崔 鸿 张海珠 主编 36元

新理念生物教学论（第二版）
崔 鸿 郑晓慧 主编 45元

新理念地理教学论（第二版） 李家清 主编 45元
新理念历史教学论（第二版） 杜 芳 主编 33元

新理念思想政治（品德）教学论（第二版）
胡田庚 主编 36元

新理念信息技术教学论（第二版）
吴军其 主编 32元

新理念数学教学论 冯 虹 主编 36元

21世纪教师教育系列教材·语文课程与教学论系列

语文文本解读实用教程 荣维东 主编 49元

语文课程教师专业技能训练
张学凯 刘丽丽 主编 45元

语文课程与教学发展简史
武玉鹏 王从华 黄修志 主编 38元

语文课程学与教的心理学基础 韩雪屏 王朝霞 主编
语文课程名师名课案例分析 武玉鹏 郭治锋 主编
语用性质的语文课程与教学论 王元华 著 42元

21世纪教师教育系列教材·学科教学技能训练系列

新理念生物教学技能训练（第二版） 崔 鸿 33元

新理念思想政治（品德）教学技能训练（第二版）
胡田庚 赵海山 29元

新理念地理教学技能训练 李家清 32元
新理念化学教学技能训练（第二版） 王后雄 36元
新理念数学教学技能训练 王光明 36元
新理念小学音乐教学法 吴跃跃 主编 38元

王后雄教师教育系列教材

教育考试的理论与方法 王后雄 主编 35元
化学教育测量与评价 王后雄 主编 45元
中学化学实验教学研究 王后雄 主编 32元
新理念化学教学诊断学 王后雄 主编 48元

西方心理学名著译丛

荣格心理学七讲 [美] 卡尔文·霍尔 45元

拓扑心理学原理 [德] 库尔德·勒温 32元
系统心理学：绪论 [美] 爱德华·铁钦纳 30元
社会心理学导论 [美] 威廉·麦独孤 36元
思维与语言 [俄] 列夫·维果茨基 30元
人类的学习 [美] 爱德华·桑代克 30元
基础与应用心理学 [德] 雨果·闵斯特伯格 36元
记忆 [德] 赫尔曼·艾宾浩斯 著 32元
儿童的人格形成及其培养 [奥地利] 阿德勒 著 35元
幼儿的感觉与意志 [德] 威廉·蒲莱尔 著 45元
实验心理学（上下册）
[美] 伍德沃斯 施洛斯贝格 著 150元
格式塔心理学原理 [美] 库尔特·考夫卡 75元
动物和人的目的性行为 [美] 爱德华·托尔曼 44元
西方心理学史大纲 唐钺 42元

心理学视野中的文学丛书

围城内外——西方经典爱情小说的进化心理学透视
熊哲宏 32元
我爱故我在——西方文学大师的爱情与爱情心理学
熊哲宏 32元

21世纪教学活动设计案例精选丛书（禹明 主编）

初中语文教学活动设计案例精选 23元
初中数学教学活动设计案例精选 30元
初中科学教学活动设计案例精选 27元
初中历史与社会教学活动设计案例精选 30元
初中英语教学活动设计案例精选 26元
初中思想品德教学活动设计案例精选 20元
中小学音乐教学活动设计案例精选 27元
中小学体育（体育与健康）教学活动设计案例精选
25元
中小学美术教学活动设计案例精选 34元
中小学综合实践活动教学活动设计案例精选 27元
小学语文教学活动设计案例精选 29元
小学数学教学活动设计案例精选 33元
小学科学教学活动设计案例精选 32元
小学英语教学活动设计案例精选 25元
小学品德与生活（社会）教学活动设计案例精选
24元
幼儿教育教学活动设计案例精选 39元

全国高校网络与新媒体专业规划教材

文化产业概论 尹章池 38元
网络文化教程 李文明 42元
网络与新媒体评论 杨娟 38元
新媒体概论 尹章池 39元
新媒体视听节目制作 周建青 45元
融合新闻学 石长顺 39元
新媒体网页设计与制作 惠悲荷 39元
网络新媒体实务 张合斌 39元
突发新闻教程 李军 45元
视听新媒体节目制作 周建青 45元
视听评论 何志武 32元
出镜记者案例分析 刘静 邓秀军 39元
视听新媒体导论 郭小平 39元
网络与新媒体广告 尚恒志 张合斌 49元
网络与新媒体文学 唐东堰 雷奕 49元

全国高校广播电视专业规划教材

电视节目策划教程 项仲平 著 36元
电视导播教程 程晋 编著 39元
电视文艺创作教程 王建辉 编著 39元
广播剧创作教程 王国臣 编著 36元

21世纪教育技术学精品教材（张景中 主编）

教育技术学导论（第二版）
李芒 金林 编著 38元
远程教育原理与技术 王继新 张屹 编著 41元
教学系统设计理论与实践 杨九民 梁林梅 编著 29元
信息技术教学论 雷体南 叶良明 主编 29元
网络教育资源设计与开发 刘清堂 主编 30元
学与教的理论与方式 刘雍潜 32元
信息技术与课程整合（第二版）
赵呈领 杨琳 刘清堂 39元
教育技术研究方法 张屹 黄磊 38元
教育技术项目实践 潘克明 32元

21世纪信息传播实验系列教材（徐福荫 黄慕雄 主编）

多媒体软件设计与开发 32元
电视照明·电视音乐音响 26元
播音与主持艺术（第二版） 38元
广告策划与创意 26元
摄影基础（第二版） 32元

21世纪教师教育系列教材·专业养成系列（赵国栋 主编）

微课与慕课设计初级教程 40元
微课与慕课设计高级教程 48元
微课、翻转课堂和慕课设计实操教程 188元
网络调查研究方法概论（第二版） 49元
PPT云课堂教学法 88元